Communications
in Computer and Information Science   1820

Rationale

The CCIS series is devoted to the publication of proceedings of computer science conferences. Its aim is to efficiently disseminate original research results in informatics in printed and electronic form. While the focus is on publication of peer-reviewed full papers presenting mature work, inclusion of reviewed short papers reporting on work in progress is welcome, too. Besides globally relevant meetings with internationally representative program committees guaranteeing a strict peer-reviewing and paper selection process, conferences run by societies or of high regional or national relevance are also considered for publication.

Topics

The topical scope of CCIS spans the entire spectrum of informatics ranging from foundational topics in the theory of computing to information and communications science and technology and a broad variety of interdisciplinary application fields.

Information for Volume Editors and Authors

Publication in CCIS is free of charge. No royalties are paid, however, we offer registered conference participants temporary free access to the online version of the conference proceedings on SpringerLink (http://link.springer.com) by means of an http referrer from the conference website and/or a number of complimentary printed copies, as specified in the official acceptance email of the event.

CCIS proceedings can be published in time for distribution at conferences or as postproceedings, and delivered in the form of printed books and/or electronically as USBs and/or e-content licenses for accessing proceedings at SpringerLink. Furthermore, CCIS proceedings are included in the CCIS electronic book series hosted in the SpringerLink digital library at http://link.springer.com/bookseries/7899. Conferences publishing in CCIS are allowed to use Online Conference Service (OCS) for managing the whole proceedings lifecycle (from submission and reviewing to preparing for publication) free of charge.

Publication process

The language of publication is exclusively English. Authors publishing in CCIS have to sign the Springer CCIS copyright transfer form, however, they are free to use their material published in CCIS for substantially changed, more elaborate subsequent publications elsewhere. For the preparation of the camera-ready papers/files, authors have to strictly adhere to the Springer CCIS Authors' Instructions and are strongly encouraged to use the CCIS LaTeX style files or templates.

Abstracting/Indexing

CCIS is abstracted/indexed in DBLP, Google Scholar, EI-Compendex, Mathematical Reviews, SCImago, Scopus. CCIS volumes are also submitted for the inclusion in ISI Proceedings.

How to start

To start the evaluation of your proposal for inclusion in the CCIS series, please send an e-mail to ccis@springer.com.

María José Abásolo · Carlos de Castro Lozano ·
Gonzalo F. Olmedo Cifuentes
Editors

Applications and Usability of Interactive TV

11th Iberoamerican Conference, jAUTI 2022
Cordoba, Spain, November 17–18, 2022
Revised Selected Papers

 Springer

Editors
María José Abásolo
Faculty of Informatic
National University of La Plata
La Plata, Argentina

Carlos de Castro Lozano
University of Córdoba
Córdoba, Spain

Gonzalo F. Olmedo Cifuentes 🆔
ESPE
Sangolquí, Ecuador

ISSN 1865-0929   ISSN 1865-0937 (electronic)
Communications in Computer and Information Science
ISBN 978-3-031-45610-7   ISBN 978-3-031-45611-4 (eBook)
https://doi.org/10.1007/978-3-031-45611-4

This Springer imprint is published by the registered company Springer Nature Switzerland AG
The registered company address is: Gewerbestrasse 11, 6330 Cham, Switzerland

Paper in this product is recyclable.

Preface

The XI Ibero-American Conference on Applications and Usability of Interactive Digital Television (jAUTI 2022) was jointly organized by CITEC of the University of Córdoba (Spain) and RedAUTI (Thematic Network on Applications and Usability of Interactive Digital Television). This conference took place from November 17 to 18, 2022, in the city of Córdoba (Spain), conducted in an online format. This book contains a collection of 9 papers referring to the design, development, and user experiences of applications for Interactive Digital Television and related technologies that were selected from 25 papers received at the event after a peer-review process; they were later extended and underwent a second peer-review process.

María José Abásolo
Carlos de Castro Lozano
Gonzalo F. Olmedo Cifuentes

Organization

General Chairs

Carlos De Castro Lozano — University of Córdoba, Spain
María José Abásolo — National University of La Plata, Argentina
Gonzalo Olmedo Cifuentes — Universidad de las Fuerzas Armadas ESPE, Ecuador

Scientific Committee

Alcina Prata — Polytechnic Institute of Setúbal, Portugal
Ana Velhinho — University of Aveiro, Portugal
Anelise Jantsch — Federal University of Rio Grande do Sul, Brazil
Antoni Oliver — University of the Balearic Islands, Spain
Beatriz Sainz de Abajo — University of Valladolid, Spain
Cecilia Sanz — National University of La Plata, Argentina
Cristina Manresa Yee — University of Balearic Islands, Spain
Diego Villamarín — Universidad de las Fuerzas Armadas ESPE, Ecuador

Douglas Paredes — University of the Andes, Venezuela
Fernanda Chocrón — Federal University of Rio Grande do Sul, Brazil
Fernando Boronat — Polytechnic University of Valencia, Spain
Francisco Montero Simarro — University of Castilla-La Mancha, Spain
Israel González Carrasco — University Carlos III, Spain
Joaquín Danilo Pina Amargós — CUJAE, Cuba
Jorge Abreu — University of Aveiro, Portugal
José Maria Buades Rubio — University of Balearic Islands, Spain
Julio Larco — Universidad de las Fuerzas Armadas ESPE, Ecuador

Manuel González Hidalgo — University of Balearic Islands, Spain
Miguel Angel Rodrigo Alonso — University of Córdoba, Spain
Patrícia Oliveira — University of Aveiro, Portugal
Pedro Almeida — University of Aveiro, Portugal
Raisa Socorro Llanes — CUJAE, Cuba
Raoni Kulesza — Federal University of Paraíba, Brazil
Rita Oliveira — University of Aveiro, Portugal
Rita Santos — University of Aveiro, Portugal

Sandra Baldassarri   University of Zaragoza, Spain
Telmo Silva   University of Aveiro, Portugal
Vagner Beserra   University of Tarapacá, Chile
Valdecir Becker   Federal University of Paraíba, Brazil

Contents

Content Creation and Interaction

Personalized Web-Based Contents, Generated Through a Cross-Media Environment, as Additional Information to Documentary Videos

Alcina Prata[1(✉)], Teresa Chambel[2], and Jorge Ferraz de Abreu[3]

[1] Superior School of Technology (ESTS), Polytechnic Institute of Setubal, Setúbal, Portugal
alcina.prata@estsetubal.ips.pt
[2] Lasige, Faculty of Sciences, University of Lisbon, Lisbon, Portugal
mtchambel@ciencias.ulisboa.pt
[3] Digimedia, Department of Communication and Arts, University of Aveiro, Aveiro, Portugal
jfa@ua.pt

Abstract. Due to their characteristics and capability to support a diversity of contexts of use through flexible solutions, cross-media environments have been gaining space with iTV being an obligatory part of these environments due to its characteristics. This paper briefly addresses the design challenges that need to be considered in the design of cross-media environments capable of generating personalized web-based contents as additional information to video, from different devices. The system designed to illustrate our research, and which evolved from previous versions, is called eiTV and generates a cross-media personalized web-based content, which provides extra information about users' selected topics of interest while watching a specific video from a documentary genre. The web-based content may be generated, accessed, personalized, shared, enriched and (immediately or later) viewed through iTV, PC and mobile phone depending on the users' needs. This paper main focus is on the 'Create functionality' wich includes the interfaces designed to generate the web content, and the 'Chat functionality' designed to support users comunication needs while watching videos, and enrich the web content. An evaluation, with the participation of 30 elements, from 16 to 52 years old, was carried out with high fidelity prototypes and the achieved results were very optimistic.

Keywords: Cross-media · Transmedia · Video · Web-content · iTV

1 Introduction

Due to their characteristics and capability to support a diversity of context of use through flexible solutions, cross-media and transmedia environments, systems and applications have been gaining space in practically all areas [10, 19, 25]. While cross-media systems refer to those where the same message is distributed through different channels/platforms (the keyword is repetition), on transmedia systems, the message is expanded through

M. J. Abásolo et al. (Eds.): jAUTI 2022, CCIS 1820, pp. 3–19, 2023.
https://doi.org/10.1007/978-3-031-45611-4_1

different devices/platforms (the keyword is expansion) [19, 25]. The success and adoption of cross-media and transmedia environments is propelled by many factors as the proliferation of new and appealing devices, technological advances, viewers change in technological interests and habits and the systems characteristics, which the most relevant are, flexibility and mobility, so essential to support today's lifestyle [10]. Our world is increasingly cross-media, and one area that benefited from these systems was learning [2–4, 26], very important considering that, lifelong learning became the new way of life.

When it comes to the medium used to support learning through cross-media systems, video is one of the richest ones. In what relates to the devices used to access videos (as even the TV consumption) it is spread amongst many different devices [7, 15]. However, the devices used to access the video, TV, PC, and mobile devices, are the privileged ones depending, mostly on the age range. Through structure and interaction, these devices can open the door to flexible environments. However, the design of these cross-media environments/systems faces some challenges that may affect their effective use and need to be addressed [12].

The eiTV system designed and developed to illustrate our research, has been through an evolution process of 4 generations of prototypes, all ranging from low to high fidelity prototypes. The fourth-generation prototypes, briefly presented in this paper, were the richer ones in terms of devices and functionalities involved, which increased to match a more flexible perspective. Running from iTV, PC and mobile phones, it provides users with the possibility to choose, from a video, which topics they would want to know more about and with which level of detail. They may decide when and where they would want to access those extra related contents (which we also refer to as informal learning environments) which are generated from iTV, PC and mobile phones, and are presented through the form of an editable and sharable web-based content. The architecture and the main features available in iTV, PC and mobile contexts were already explored and described in previous publications [1–4]. After the excellent results achieved with the third-generation prototypes (where the videos were from the well-known series CSI), the fourth generation were conceptualized and developed to provide continuity to the research opportunities identified [4]. From the research opportunities identified, we have considered that, two of them, the use of documentary videos (videos typically more dynamic and that by its nature are typically watched in a lean forward mode) and social communication tools, would have a better chance to succeed if implemented together. In fact, the existence of social communication tools was anchored in the use of documentary videos, resulting in a return of '1 + 1 > 2' as we have envisioned and was later confirmed through the evaluation process.

After this introduction, Sect. 2 includes a review of related work and concepts, Sect. 3 describes the design challenges of cross-media applications in that context, Sect. 4 presents some of the most important design decisions, Sect. 5 describes the evaluation process and, finally, Sect. 6 presents the conclusions and perspectives for future research and developments.

2   Related Work

This section addresses some of the more relevant related research studies in cross-media environments that include the same or similar devices and/or have informal/formal learning goals and uses integrated social communication tools.

The TAMALLE project [20] developed a 'dual device system' for informal English language learning, based on watching iTV and selecting what to access later on mobile phones. This was an interesting system capable to accommodate different cognitive modes and different contexts of use, especially, if considering the mobile phone possibilities. Obrist et al. [23] developed a "6 key navigation model" and its interface for an electronic program guide running on the TV, PC and mobile phone. The different devices were not used in a complementary way since the intention was to test a similar interface, on three different devices. They have perceived that viewers prefer fewer navigation keys and a unified UI with the same functionalities across devices. This confirmed our prototypes UI design last decisions. Newstream [24] provides extra information about what is being watched and related websites, using TV, PC and mobiles. Depending on the viewers' needs, that extra information may be viewed immediately, stored for later view or pushed to other device. Each device maintains awareness of each other and are able to: move interaction to the device that makes the most sense in a specific context, use several devices simultaneously, and use the mobile device as a remote to the TV and PC. Limitations include: the system relies almost exclusively on social networks to receive and share content, for interaction and dialogues; and the limited viewer direct influence on the new contents presented as extra information. Our work is more flexible in these concerns. 2BEON [13], currently called WeOnTV is, an iTV application which supports the communication between viewers, textually and in real time, while watching a specific program. It also allows viewers to see which of their contacts are online, which programs they are watching, and instant messaging on the iTV, demonstrated to be important to give viewers a sense of presence and was implemented with smartphones as "secondary input devices". This work demonstrates the importance of sharing information with viewers' contacts about what they are watching on TV, which supports our own decision of including a sharing functionality in eiTV. Cronkite [18] provides extra information to viewers of broadcast news. While viewers are watching a news story, they feel the need to know more about it, they press the "interest" button on their remote and the system provides them with extra information on the computer display. The extra information, is about the story that they are watching rather than specific topics of interest inside the story, which is somehow limited. To have the system working, both TV and PC need to be simultaneously on. The system is limited considering that the extra information is not stored for latter view (and that might be the viewers' preference). Our application stores the related information for later use, the simultaneous use of iTV and PC is a possibility but not the only option, viewers may select very specific topics of interest inside a story instead of the whole story and some specific functionalities, as asynchronous communication tools, were also contemplated.

3 Cross-Media Design Challenges

This section describes the key aspects, cognitive and affective, that need to be considered to effectively design cross-media environments and interfaces, with a special focus on the design challenges associated with video and different devices.

Media and Cognition. Norman's view [8] defines two fundamental cognitive modes. The experiential mode allows us to perceive and react to events naturally and without cognition, but require different technological support, and the medium affects the way we interpret and use the message and its impact on us. To exemplify, TV and video are typically watched in an experiential mode while learning strongly relies on reflection. A successful integration of media should have into account what each medium and device is most suited for in each context of use, augmenting and complementing their capabilities in a flexible combination.

Cross-Media Interaction, Conceptual Model and User Experience. The main challenges of cross-media interaction design described by [17] include: consistency, interoperability, and technological literacy needed for the different devices. The conceptual model, how the software will look like and act, is also a very important aspect since several interaction scenarios and contexts are involved [9]. The quality of the interaction cannot be measured only by the quality of the system parts, but as a whole. In this context, the user experience (UX) may be evaluated through how well it supports the synergic use of each medium and the different kinds of affordances involved, also understanding what makes the user pass the current medium boundaries to use other media as well. According to [16], the UX may involve the isolated perception of the medium (distributed), one of the biggest barriers to its efficient use and adoption, or the perception of the system as a whole unity (coherent). According to [23], the UX evaluation methods and measures relevant, when ubiquitous TV is involved, are: physiological data; data mining, log files, observation, case studies, lab experiments, experience sampling method, probes, diaries, interviews, surveys and focus groups. The combination of methods to use depends on each specific case.

Supporting Cross-Media HCI. In this context, the migration of tasks is supported via cross-media usability and continuity, influencing on how well and smoothly users' skills and experiences are transferred across the different devices [21] and contexts of use. The consistent look and feel across media is an important requirement, even if it should not limit the goal of having each medium doing what it is most suited for and extending its characteristics (synergic use) [11].

Designing for Different Devices and Contexts of Use. Cross-media design involves designing interfaces for different devices. To understand the devices and have each one doing what it is most suited for, the best approach is usually to study each particular situation, including device characteristics and cognitive and affective aspects associated to its use: why people use them, in which mode, compare them, etc., and the design guidelines for each device [1] followed by an adequate combination.

Supporting Communication tools in Cross-media contexts. The use of communication tools integrated with cross-media contexts and environments requires the understanding of each device and media characteristics. Each device should contribute with what is most suited for while the media should not change its nature by the incrementation of new tools. Every type of communication tool, in this context, should be designed mainly with UX in mind. To minimize the complexity associated to this type of contexts and take the best advantage on the users' previous knowledge, the Interface should be as close as possible from the more traditional use given to that kind of tool (if an already existent one is being replicated in a different device) [4].

4 Cross-Media Design in eiTV

In brief, this Section presents main functionalities and design options concerning the eiTV Cross-media system, in response to the challenges identified in Sect. 3. A specific focus was given to the Create and Chat functionalities considering that it refers to what's new on this paper.

4.1 eiTV Architecture

The eiTV system is a portal aggregator of all the functionalities which may be accessed from any of the devices (iTV, PC and mobile phones) thus working as a true 'ecosystem of devices'. Through the portal we may: generate web contents; see, edit and share web contents, upload files, change profile, etc. In sum, everyone may receive web contents generated by the eiTV, a characteristic that provides **flexibility** to the application.

4.2 Flexible Navigation Model

We opted for a menu style navigation which provides **users** much more **control** over their choices, considering that all the functionalities may be accessed at any moment, directly through the menu or through the chromatic keys. This model improves: the application **interoperability** since it shows people how it works; the **UX** which becomes more **coherent** considering that users easily perceive the system as a whole unit; the **cross-media interaction continuity** through different devices and the **interaction consistency** considering that it becomes easier to reuse users interaction knowledge. Due to its **flexibility** this model is also more adapted to changes **in cognition modes,** levels of **attention** and technological **literacy.**

4.3 Flexible Navigation Model

a) The **Create functionality** allows users to watch videos and select topics of interest for further information. The selectable topics appear underlined in the subtitles (see Fig. 1 a) and for the first time, due to the nature and characteristics of the videos being used (documentary), each line may contain one selectable topic. Let's imagine the traditional subtitle with 2 lines. The first line selectable topic appears in a bright white color for a few seconds, then it becomes grey (signaling that is no longer selectable, at least at that moment) and the second line topic is the one that becomes bright white.

The selected topics change their color to red and a little box with a ✔ inside, appears in front of the line where the selected topic is, in order to create visual feedback on the users selected topics. When the videos being watched don't have subtitles, only the selectable topic words appear onscreen to let the users know which topics may be selected. As to the information about a topic, three levels were proposed, from less to high informative (as presented in Table 1):

Table 1 Levels of information about a topic

Level	Description/Ambit	Interface:
Level 1 (topics)	Only implies the use of the designed solutions in order to select topics of interest	1. remote OK button when watching the video from the TV 2. to touch the screen (when watching the video from the mobile) 3. use the mouse or touch the screen when watching from the PC)
Level 2 (summary)	Implies the immediate display of extra information as a brief summary about the topics	The immediate extra information appears: 1. overlaid onscreen or 2. embedded onscreen
Level 3 (structured)	Implies the immediate display of extra information, namely a structured list of that topic main aspects or options that the user may choose	The immediate extra information appears: 1. overlaid onscreen or 2. embedded onscreen

At any moment, the user can change between levels of information by pressing button 1, 2 or 3 or by using the directional buttons or by using the mouse or touch screen (depending on the device being used). Thus, the eiTV navigation is adaptable to users with different technological literacy. It was decided to maintain the 3 levels of information (see Fig. 1 – a, bottom bar: where the 3 levels are represented and level 2 can be seen as the one selected), with embedded and overlaid options on levels 2 and 3, since we saw from the previous prototypes, that they play an important role to accommodate viewers' changes in cognition modes, levels of attention, goals, needs and interaction preferences. These options also give users the possibility to personalize their viewing/interactive model, so important when video is involved [6].

As to the personalized generated web-based content, its structure particularities are described nex:

My Input. Each web content is organized as follows. The left side menu contains all the topics selected by the user, presented by the order of selection in the video, to improve contextualization, but the user may choose to see them by alphabetical or logical (content

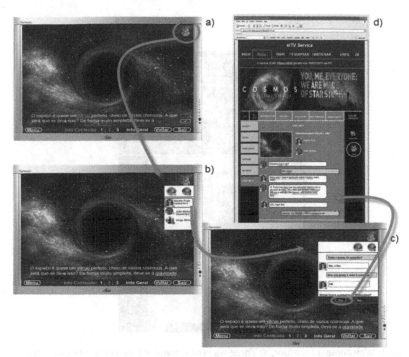

Fig. 1. a) Chat icon on the right corner of the video; b) List of users that use the eiTV system (with the green bullet to show the ones online and the red bullet to show the ones offline); c) Chat messages changed between 2 users and the button to save those messages on the web content; d) Chat messages saved on the web content specific 'CHAT input' place.

dependent) order (see Fig. 2 – a). This option was designed to take advantage of each device characteristics to provide flexibility.

CHAT Input. On the web content left side menu, bellow the 'My input' place there is the 'CHAT Input' place (see Fig. 2 – b) where the chat conversations that took place inside the system are saved and presented (if the user decides to store them), see Fig. 1 - d. The description of the chat functionality is presented in g). This functionality was made available to provide users with more flexibility and to support their social communication needs without losing the sense of unity (considering that they didn't need to use external means and devices to communicate, just the ones included in the eiTV system in a specific an integrated way). As to the interaction model and interfaces (see Fig. 1 – c, d), they were designed considering the UX and the devices and media characteristics in order to have each device contributing with its strongest features.

Editing. Each web content has the possibility to be edited. This edition ranges from uploading textual information (if through the TV set) or textual information and files (if through PC or mobile phones) or GPS coordinates (if through the mobile phones), to delete, move, edit, import or define privacy status of the web content, a topic of the web content, a category from a specific topic (see Fig. 2 - c), etc. This provides flexibility,

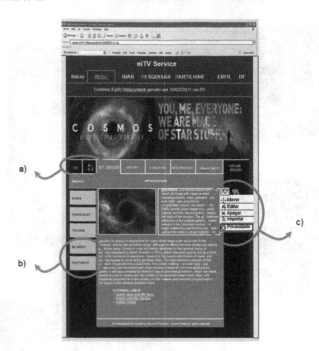

Fig. 2. eiTV Web content Interface. a) Three ways of organizing the selected topics; b) 'My input' and 'CHAT input' web content places; c) some web content editing possibilities.

control, consistent interaction and takes advantage of each device characteristics and UX.

Continuity and Contextualization. The web content continuity and contextualization, was supported via the use of some excerpts from the original video, namely, the excerpts that were being watched in the moment of the topic selection.

b) **Search functionality** allows searching videos based on different criteria, namely, video criteria: title, actor name, etc.; and system criteria: video with or without web content(s) already generated. This provides **flexibility.**

c) The **Share functionality** is activated only after users accessed the Create or Search functionalities. The share functionality allows sharing the generated web content or retrieved video (with or without web content), with their contacts. On this functionality flexibility and error prevention were improved.

d) The **User Profile functionality** allows to upload users' personal data from their social networks, allows validation, etc. The user profile information is used to personalize the web content, thus improving **flexibility**.

e) The **DF functionality** was designed to have each device doing what it is most suited for. To achieve this goal, **contexts of use**, **device characteristics** and **cognitive and affective aspects** associated to the devices use, were studied. In the case of mobile phones functionalities, the following were made available:

e1) Great flexibility and mobility (use it everywhere, anytime, anyway): When using the TV, the scroll is not an option, but that does not happen when using the other devices; contrary to TV and PC, mobile phones are easily used everywhere, even when users are standing up, meaning that any extra time may be used.

e2) Location-based search using the GPS functionality: The search functionality allows users to search videos and images related to their current location (see Fig. 3). As an example, when near the NASA building the user may use this functionality to search, from its own system and the internet, videos and images related to that specific spot (this type of video files need to be inserted when using iTV or PC);

e3) Add immediately, or latter, shot pictures or videos, that may be related to the video being watched, as additional information to the web content or, instead, really integrated as part of the wcb content.

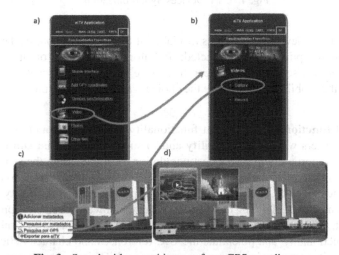

Fig. 3. Search videos and images from GPS coordinates.

Video capture and location-based search: a) Options available at the DF functionality and 'Video' option being activated; b) Possibility to choose from a video gallery or to record a new video. The user chose one video from the gallery; c) The user is choosing to search related videos and images (related to the one that was chosen through the gallery) by GPS coordinates; d) The two results – one video (on the left side) and one photo (on the right side) recorded in very close places - appear as thumbnails embedded in the video chosen from the gallery. A simple click on the video allows to watch it.

f) The **Devices Synchronization functionality** - The possibility to synchronize devices was designed and implemented to allow the application to work as a true ecosystem of devices. Figure 4 illustrates this option via mobile phone. When accessed through PC and TV, the same interfaces are available. Only the interface presented in Fig. 4 - a) changes considering that 'Add GPS coordinates' it is a mobile phone specific option.

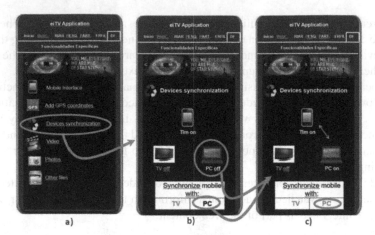

Fig. 4. eiTV Devices Synchronization.

Synchronizing devices: a) Options available at the DF functionality. The 'Devices Synchronization' option is being selected; b) Automatic detection on the system connected interfaces. Users using the menu to choose with which device(s) they want to synchronize the mobile; c) In this case the choice was with the PC (the only device that was on).

g) The **Chat functionality** – the chat functionality was designed and made available to provide users with more **flexibility** and to support their **social communication needs** (so important on the youngest population) without losing the sense of **unity** (considering that they don't need to use external means and devices to communicate, just the ones included in the eiTV system in a specific an integrated way) as will be explained next. After logging in, and unless they specifically decide to appear offline, by default, users will appear online to all the others. To facilitate the learning and use of this functionality, and potentiate the **UX**, references and characteristics common to other similar communication tools were followed. Thus, users may personalize the chat with their pictures (like it happens in WhatsApp, messenger, etc.). When online, users have a small green bullet associated with the picture (like on Instagram, etc.) and when offline users have a small red bullet associated with the picture (like on TEAMS), Fig. 1 - b. There is an icon on the right corner of the video (see Fig. 1 – a). When the users choice is to enter in offline mode, this icon will be available onscreen only for the first 3 min of the video, next disappearing until activated again through a specific key on the remote (when watching the video through the TV set), through a simple touch on the video (when watching the video through the mobile phone) and through a click/touch on the icon (when watching the video through the PC). At any time, users may see the list of other users that also use the system, choose one or more, and start interacting through a chat conversation. The messages appear on the right corner of the screen (Fig. 1 – c) with the indentation typically used on other communication tools (the sent messages appear aligned to the right while the received messages appear aligned to the left and with the user picture, similarly to what happens with the messenger, Instagram, WhatsApp, etc.). These design options help reduce the learning curve and take the best advantage of the UX. Important to refer that when the user is watching the video through the TV and activates the chat option, the devices synchronization functionality (already described in f) is automatically activated and synchronizes the TV set with the mobile device. From then, the mobile device is prepared to be used as a 'keyboard' to the messages that will appear on the TV screen. This option improves the system **usability** (considering that writing through a TV remote is a very difficult and time-consuming task), takes the best advantage of each **device characteristics** and, once again, the system works in an **integrated** way as a true **ecosystem of devices** providing users with a sense of unity and continuity. When a user receives messages, a 'pause option' automatically appears onscreen. This option gives users the possibility to pause the video, right away or later, and focus on answering the chat messages without losing the video content and the opportunity to choose topics of interest. When the user is watching the video through the other two devices (mobile or PC) and activates the chat option, the devices synchronization is not activated considering that the devices in use have suitable keyboards to write the messages and don't need extra resources to improve usability. Important to note that the chat option was made available only during the visualization of the video, thus giving support to the users' socialization needs. Its usual to see these socialization needs arise during video watching, not only due to the video's dynamic nature, but because socialization it's a phenomenon pretty much associated to the TV consumption which typically occurs in group. It is normal to share and comment with others what we are watching, mainly if it is news, sports or documentary related. When users ask to exit the chat, by default the system asks if they want to save the conversations. If the answer is yes, the messages are stored in the web content, in the 'CHAT input' area (see Fig. 1– d), thus providing users with more flexibility and personalization possibilities. Important to note that the chat may be used in any circumstance while watching a video. However, to save the chat conversations is only possible after choosing the first topic of interest, which is the action that makes possible later generate a related web content.

Consistency in UX and the perception of the system coherent unity independently of the device being used was also a priority. Despite having considered the mobile device characteristics and contexts of use in the design, towards a more simplified design, we decided to keep a coherent layout in terms of colors, symbols and other graphic elements, as navigational buttons, in order to better contextualize users, give them a sense of unity in their UX and to allow a smooth transition among media and devices. This way, it was possible to provide users with a sense of sequence and continuity, respect the context of use and be consistent in terms of look and feel and navigational options in all the devices, and to help in the perception of the application as a unity. Users are aware that they may access their eiTV system through different devices whenever they create web contents, helping to conceptually understand the system as an 'ecosystem of devices'.

5 Evaluation

The UX evaluation is important in any type of system and context [14]. The UX methods and measures considered relevant for this specific case were: observation, case studies, lab experiments, experience sampling method, questionnaire, interviews and focus groups. In what relates to the design of the new functionalities and interfaces, 3 usability experts were consulted. As to the final evaluation, which occurred from February to November 2021, there were 30 participants, ranging from 16 to 52 years old, which were grouped into 2 evaluation groups: Group 1 (G1) composed of 15 participants, aged between 18 and 52 who already participated on previous evaluations and Group 2 (G2) composed of 15 participants, aged between 16 and 43 who were never in contact with the eiTV system. Inside each group the participants were categorized into 3 subgroups as follows: 5 with high technological literacy; 5 with medium technological literacy and 5 with poor technological literacy. Each subgroup was composed of 1 person with less than 25 years old, 2 persons between 25 and 40, and 2 persons with more than 40. As to the participants technological literacy categorization, it was possible via the use of a questionnaire with questions as: do you use Internet? e-mail? Facebook? Instagram? WhatsApp? How many hours a day? From which devices? etc. The idea of using a group of evaluators that already participated on previous evaluations was to understand to what extend this system resulted more complex and/or hard to use when compared with the previous versions. The idea of using a group of evaluators that never interacted with the system was to try to perceive how easy, useful, interesting it was for them, how usable the interfaces were and, amongst other factors, what impact the application had on them, particularly, considering this new level of complexity. The evaluation process started with a demonstration of the high-fidelity prototype using the three devices involved (iTV, PC and mobile phone) and the functionalities being tested. Then, users were asked to perform tasks that allowed us to evaluate:

a) the specific interfaces created for choosing topics of interest, from the three devices, while watching documentary videos;
b) the communication tool (chat) functionality interfaces designed for the three devices, and this functionality interest.

The mentioned tasks were performed in three different contextual scenarios using three different devices: at a simulated 'living room', each user used the iTV to visualize the documentary videos, generate a web content and used the chat to communicate with other testers that were online (each user was in the living room alone). Next, users went to the library which, although surrounded by people, is a quiet place and a context that replicates the scenario of a medical waiting room. Here they used the PC to watch new documentary videos, generate a web content and use the chat. Next, they moved to the school bar and repeated the previous tasks but through the mobile device. Finally, users were asked to fill a questionnaire and were interviewed. The questionnaire was based on the USE questionnaire (usefulness, satisfaction, and ease of use) [5]; the NASA TLX questionnaire (cognitive overload) [22]; and usability heuristics. Independently of the group, medium and high technological literacy categories reacted well to difficulties. However, when considering low technological literacy categories, it was possible to see that, as expected, in the presence of difficulties, the 2 older participants from G2 reacted with higher resistance and discouragement than G1. From Table 2 it is possible to see that, for both groups, the PC is the preferred device to generate the web content (G1 – 40%; G2 – 47%). As to the second preferred device, G1 chose mobile (33%) while G2 chose iTV (33%). These results were somehow unexpected but, from the observation and qualitative evaluation it was possible to perceive that both groups considered the iTV interfaces well designed and intuitive. G2 chose the iTV as their second preferred device to choose topics of interest (33%), instead of the mobile (contrary to what happened with G1). This was more visible in the categories with poor and medium technological literary. It makes sense considering that even with the need to back forward some videos they feel more comfortable using iTV than mobile phones. Anyway, this is a good indicator considering that G2 was testing the prototype for the first time and with a higher level of interface complexity when compared to previous evaluations. This indicates that the iTV interaction was well designed and that users are becoming more comfortable in what relates to interact with the TV set. However, the major critic was about the difficulty that they felt in choosing topics of interest on time, mainly when from iTV. In fact, now there are 2 topics on each 'subtitle sequence' so the time to choose a topic was reduced to half (when compared to previous scenarios when there was only one eligible topic). The problem was not the increased complexity itself, not even the selected topics feedback (which was considered good through all devices), but the necessity of a faster reaction and response. Some users had to pause the video and back forward to be able to select the topic on interest. That solution worked but, with some level of frustration when repeated several times. Thus, something needs to be done to solve this constraint, namely, rethink and improve the interfaces and consider and explore new ways of input. Another critic was about the red color used to show that the topics were selected. The users (G1 - 33%; G2 – 40%) argued that they first reaction was that they had made something wrong and that the red color indicated some sort of warning.

Table 2 Preferred Device to Generate the Web Content

Device to generate the Web Content	G1	G2
iTV	4 (27%)	5 (33%)
PC	6 (40%)	7 (47%)
Mobile phone	5 (33%)	3 (20%)

In terms of the chat functionality, something that was implemented on mid fidelity prototypes for the first time and was never tested before, both groups reacted well as may be seen from Table 3. However, from the qualitative evaluation it was possible to understand the weak results obtained in relation to the easiness of use. In fact, what was harder for them was the pitch used in the chat, which was considered very small to their needs. When this option was designed, we kept the chat in a small part of the top right side of the screen to avoid losing the connection with the video being watched. In fact, users could be more interested in continuing the viewing process for a while, or even until the end of the video, before answering the chat. The design of the solution needs to be adapted to improve its usability.

Table 3 Evaluation of the chat functionality

The Chat functionality:	G1	G2
Useful	15 (100%)	13 (87%)
Easy to use	11 (73%)	9 (60%)
Easy to learn	14 (93%)	13 (87%)
Like to have it	12 (80%)	13 (87%)
Recommend to a friend	13 (87%)	14 (93%)

As may be seen from Table 4, the preferred device to use the chat was the mobile phone in both groups (somehow expected due to its continuous use to send messages amongst all ages). However, one of our main goals was to perceive if having the mobile phone automatically synchronized with the iTV to serve as keyboard while using the chat was a good idea and, mainly, if it was used with success. As previously explained, the 30 participants used the chat through the three devices and, in spite not preferring the iTV to do it, the majority (80%) considered the idea of using the mobile phone as a keyboard very good, 87% considered easy to use both devices (iTV and mobile phone) simultaneously, but 60% mentioned that, in spite easy and intuitive, that kind of simultaneous use was distracting from the video being watched on the iTV.

Table 4 Preferred device to use the Chat

Preferred device to use the Chat	G1	G2
iTV	3 (20%)	2 (13%)
PC	5 (33%)	6 (40%)
Mobile phone	7 (47%)	7 (47%)

As to the intention of transmitting a sense of unity through the chat, it was achieved with success (G1: 100%; G2: 93%).

As a whole, the eiTV cross-media system was evaluated and the results are presented on Table 5.

As can be seen, the evaluation of groups G1 and G2 are close which was a very good surprise but, as expected, better in G1. As to the two users, from G2, that didn't find the system useful, there was a 16 years boy with hight technological literacy that didn't considered the system useful mainly due to the fact that he doesn't appreciate documentaries and, even if so, he considered that the system, in spite not difficult to use for him, would be very hard to use for oldest people like his grandparents. The other user, a 42 years old participant with low technological literacy, he didn't find the system useful because he prefers to search things online through is mobile device when needs extra information. In general, the results were considered very good. Important to refer

Table 5 Overall Evaluation of the Whole eiTV Cross-media

Whole Application	G1	G2
Useful	15 (100%)	13 (87%)
Easy to use	13 (87%)	11 (73%)
Easy to learn	13 (87%)	11 (73%)
Like to have it	14 (93%)	12 (80%)
Recommend to a friend	14 (93%)	13 (87%)

that educational tests were not carried out. As mentioned previously, the generated web-contents aggregate additional information based on the users topics of interest so, they may be considered informal learning environments. Thus being, assessing how learning was improved by this portal was outside the scope of our work.

6 Conclusions and Future Work

The evaluation results were very encouraging. In many aspects, the designed functionalities (Create and Chat) and the system flexibility were perceived as useful and an added value in the cross-media research area. Some design options allowed to accommodate the changes in users' cognitive mode (e.g., information levels), and the prototype was designed and tested in real scenarios and contexts of use. Considering the design framework followed, the trends in the use of multiple devices, and the results of this and previous studies, we have reasons to believe that our goal for this cross-media context is worth pursuing and that we can achieve quite good results with all the devices in different scenarios. However, this study is limited considering that only the Create and Chat functionalities were implemented and tested. Thus, as future work, we intend to improve the interfaces (mainly the iTV ones), the create functionality, the chat interface model, test de system as a whole unit, and continue exploring the devices technological advances to create new input solutions and functionalities capable to better support users needs and different cognitive modes. A continuous improvement of the interfaces, so they may become easier to learn and adopted by an elderly population, is also a goal.

References

1. Prata, A., Chambel, T.: Going beyond iTV: designing flexible video-based cross-media interactive services as informal learning contexts. In: Proceedings of 9th European Conference on Interactive TV and Video: Ubiquitous TV EuroiTV in coop with ACM, pp. 65–74, Lisbon, Portugal (2011)
2. Prata, A., Chambel, T.: Mobility in a crossmedia environment capable of generating personalized informal learning contents from iTV, pc and mobile devices. In: Proceedings of JAUTI 2019 – VIII Conferência Iberoamericana sobre Aplicações e Usabilidade da TV Interativa, pp. 59–71, Rio de Janeiro, Brasil (2019)

3. Prata, A., Chambel, T.: Mobility in crossmedia systems, the design challenges that need to be addressed. In: Abásolo, M., Kulesza, R., Pina Amargós, J. (eds.) Applications and Usability of Interactive TV. jAUTI 2019. Communications in Computer and Information Science, vol. 1202. Springer, Cham (2020). https://doi.org/10.1007/978-3-030-56574-9_5

4. Prata, A., Chambel, T.: Personalized interactive video-based crossmedia informal learning environments from iTV, pc and mobile devices – the design challenges. In: Abásolo, M. (eds.) Applications and Usability of Interactive TV. jAUTI 2020. Communications in Computer and Information Science. Springer, pp. 89–104 (2021). https://doi.org/10.1007/978-3-030-81996-5

5. Arnold Lund, A.: Measuring Usability with the USE Questionnaire (2001). https://garyperlman.com/quest/quest.cgi?form=USE. Accessed 16 June 2021

6. Cardoso, B., Abreu, J.: TV personalisation: blending linear and ondemand content in the living room. I. J. Entertain. Technol. Manage. 1(2), 162–177 (2021)

7. Cardoso, B.: A Unificação no consumo de conteúdos audiovisuais: contributos para a experiência de utilização e sugestões para operadores, PhD thesis, Communications and Arts Department, Aveiro University, 14 January 2022, Portugal (2022)

8. Norman, D.: Things that Make us Smart. Addison Wesley Publishing Company (1993)

9. Norman, D.: The Design of Everyday Things. Basic Books, New York (2002)

10. Jenkins, H.: Transmedia missionaries, Henry Jenkins (2009). http://www.youtube.com/watch?v=bhGBfuyN5gg. Accessed 19 Nov 2020

11. Nielsen, J.: Coordinating User interfaces for consistency. Neuauflage 2002 ed., the Morgan Kaufmann Series in Interactive Technologies, San Francisco, CA, USA (1989)

12. Taplin, J.: Long Time Coming: has interactive tv finally arrived? Opening keynote. In: Proceedings of 9th European Conference on Interactive TV and Video: Ubiquitous TV (EuroiTV'2011), in coop with ACM, pp. 9, Lisbon, Portugal (2011)

13. Abreu, J.: Design de Serviços e Interfaces num Contexto de Televisão Interactiva. PhD Thesis, Communications and Arts Department, Aveiro University, Portugal (2007)

14. Abreu, J., Almeida, P., Silva, T.: A UX evaluation approach for second-screen applications. In: Abásolo, M.J., Perales, F.J., Bibiloni, A. (eds.) Applications and Usability of Interactive TV, pp. 105–120. Springer International Publishing, Cham (2016). https://doi.org/10.1007/978-3-319-38907-3_9

15. Abreu, J.F., Almeida, P., Velhinho, A., Varsori, E.: Returning to the TV screen: the potential of content unification in iTV. In: Oliveira, L. (ed.) Managing Screen Time in an Online Society:, pp. 146–171. IGI Global (2019). https://doi.org/10.4018/978-1-5225-8163-5.ch007

16. Segerståhl, K., Oinas-Kukkonen, H.: Distributed User Experience in Persuasive Technology Environments. In: Y. de Kort et al. (Eds.), Lecture notes in Computer Science 4744, Persuasive 2007, Springer-Verlag (2007) https://doi.org/10.1007/978-3-540-77006-0_10

17. Segerståhl, K.: Utilization of pervasive it compromised? Understanding the adoption and use of a cross media system. In: Proceedings of 7TH International Conference on Mobile and Ubiqitous Multimedia (MUM'2008) in cooperation with ACM SIGMOBILE, pp. 168–175, Umea, Sweden (2008)

18. Livingston, K., Dredze, M., Hammond, K., Birnbaum, L.: Beyond broadcast. In: Proceedings of ACM IUI'2003, The Seventh International Conference on Intelligent User Interfaces, (Miami, USA, January 12–15, 2003), 260–262 (2003)

19. Moloney, K.: Multimedia, crossmedia, tranmedia… What's in a name? (2014). https://transmediajournalism.org/2014/04/21/multimedia-crossmedia-transmedia-whats-in-a-name/. Accessed 30 Nov 2020

20. Pemberton, L., Fallahkhair, S.: Design issues for dual device learning: interactive television and mobile phone. In: Proceedings of 4th World Conference on mLearning - Mobile Technology: the future of Learn in your hands (mLearn'2005), Cape Town, South Africa (2005)

21. Florins, M., Vanderdonckt, J.: Graceful degradation of user interfaces as a design method for multiplatform systems. In: Proceedings of the ACM International Conference on Intelligent User Interfaces (IUI'04), pp. 140–147, Funchal, Madeira (2004)

22. NASA. NASA TLX Paper and Pencil Version (2019). https://humansystems.arc.nasa.gov/groups/tlx/tlxpaperpencil.php. Accessed 16 June 2021

23. Obrist, M., Knoch, H.: How to investigate the quality of user experience for ubiquitous TV? Tutorial. In: Proceedings of EuroiTV'2011, 9th European Conference on Interactive TV and Video: Ubiquitous TV, Lisbon, Portugal (2011)

24. Martin, R., Holtzman, H.: Newstream. A multi-device, cross-medium, and socially aware approach to news content. In: Proceedimgs of 8th European Interactive TV Conference (EuroiTV 2010), in coop with ACM, pp. 83–90, Tampere, Finland (2010)

25. Gambarato, R.: Crossmedia, multimedia and transmedia. (2020). https://www.youtube.com/watch?v=G3wdbajO6js. Accessed 30 Nov 2020

26. Bonometti, S.: Learning in cross-media environment. Int. J. Web-Based Learn. Teach. Technol. **12**(4), 48–57 (2017)

MNEMOSCOPE – A Model for Digital Co-creation and Visualization of Collective Memories

Ana Velhinho$^{(\boxtimes)}$ 🆔 and Pedro Almeida 🆔

Digimedia, Department of Communication and Art, University of Aveiro, Aveiro, Portugal
{ana.velhinho,almeida}@ua.pt

Abstract. In the domain of cultural events, heritage and memory institutions, crowdsourcing and user-generated content have a growing impact on the emergence of social archives, the enrichment of digital collections and sharing of collective memories and experiences. In this context, a technology-mediated model through a participatory digital platform is proposed based on a research process comprising a multiple case study, prototype testing with users and exploratory interviews with experts. The model combines online and offline strategies, namely visualization, gamification, and locative practices, to potentiate the aggregation, correlation, and co-creation of collaborative digital resources. The participatory nature of this proposal intends to empower individuals, municipalities and cultural entities like museums, libraries, and local organizations to create and expand their community archives around past and current events, by presenting them in a multidimensional way. The model is presented through a set of operative components and principles regarding participation, visualization, and mediation, to guide the development of prototypes for specific contexts and territories. The receptivity and recommendations from potential users and experts allowed us to design the MNEMOSCOPE model in a flexible way to be adaptable and scalable. Following, the development and testing of a functional platform will be held within an R&D project, focused on cultural events and experiences in Portugal.

Keywords: Participatory platform · Digital storytelling · Social archives · Collective memory

1 Introduction

The current investigation is framed on Participatory Culture [1] in which digital storytelling [2, 3] and interactive visualizations [4–6], driven by social computing and by participatory and co-creation methodologies [7], support entertainment and creativity domains but also cultural and knowledge production [8].

Lev Manovich [5] described the impact of new media in the 21st century as a computerization of culture, which redefined the mediascape and introduced new cultural models and forms such as the database. This paradigm shift influenced the whole media cycle, further propelled by Web 2.0, facilitating content flow and production, which are

M. J. Abásolo et al. (Eds.): jAUTI 2022, CCIS 1820, pp. 20–35, 2023.
https://doi.org/10.1007/978-3-031-45611-4_2

the core of Convergence Culture [1]. Consequently, users acquire an enhanced role as *prosumers*, as they are not exclusively consumers but also contribute with their content – known as User Generated Content (UGC). In this sense, convergence is also profoundly linked to participation and building a sense of community, as people actively create and share content around a common interest, relying on a group effort.

Currently, social dynamics among online communities are intrinsic to participatory societies, increasing possibilities for inclusion through UGC and life testimonials, which are gradually becoming relevant contributions. Given the acceleration of the ongoing process of culture digitization, the construction of collective memory is significantly affected by the forms and technologies of capturing and accessing records of those memories [9, 10], which also impacts the internal workflow of memory institutions (archives, libraries, and museums).

On the one hand, this shift also influences the research field giving rise to emerging knowledge areas supported by computing and digital data processing (including big data) to study cultural processes and artefacts, namely the Digital Humanities [11] and the Cultural Analytics [12]. On the other hand, the popularization of interactive visualizations opens new possibilities for visual presentation, since the same data can be tailored to tell different stories [3, 6], providing users more control to explore, co-create, and convey group storytelling [2]. In this way, digital platforms offering exploratory interfaces [4, 13, 14] propelled by the self-organized crowd [15, 16] may motivate the sharing of multiple points of view for the digital enhancement of experiences as collective constructs.

In this context, through the proposal of a model mediated by a participatory platform, the present investigation aimed to encourage networked co-creation through the combination of digital resources to contribute to enhancing shared experiences within the domains of cultural events and intangible cultural heritage, partially dispersed or with limited access. Also, for visualizing real-time experiences in a multidimensional way and preserving them for future remembrance.

In terms of structure, the document comprises three sections: the first contextualizes the research domain; the second presents the concept and methodological approach, detailing each phase; the third presents the model and its guiding principles; and the fourth systematizes the research contributions and its continuity through future work.

2 Concept and Methodology

The concept of the participatory platform supported by the model (see Fig. 1) is giving users the autonomy to capture and share records of collective experiences to promote multiple narratives from correlated views (e.g., based on time, geolocation, semantic correlation, networks and links between users and content, etc.). This platform has the following objectives: to strengthen the participatory culture by giving people a voice through UGC; bringing cultural institutions and local associations closer to their audiences; enhance the way communities interact with places and events; aggregate and enrich multimedia records of locative experiences; explore the diversity and creativity of multiple perspectives of collective memories; and co-create a living archive based on paradigms of our time.

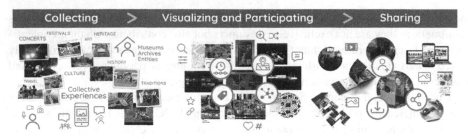

Fig. 1. Concept of the digital platform for sharing and co-creating collective memories.

The main premise for the conceptualization of the digital platform is the shared interest of people around a common goal, place, or experience so that it can reach a communal dimension. As an example, memories about a personality or collective (e.g., an artist, a band, a cultural entity, a community, etc.), a place (e.g., a monument, a city, a neighborhood, the evolution of a place or building over time, etc.), an event (a historical commemoration, a music festival, an academic festivity, a collective trip, etc.) or a know-how process (e.g. a craft activity, a local tradition, etc.). Another requirement for the platform is the digital nature of the records uploaded by users accompanied by metadata to enable aggregation and correlated visualization. Hence, the resulting indexed collections and their potential for establishing connections and generating storytelling may constitute valuable and enhanced resources for entities, researchers, and audiences, either as initiators or followers of 'memory projects' available on the digital platform.

Regarding the methodology, the investigation [17] developed an empirical study with an exploratory and qualitative approach centred on the Grounded Theory [18], which feeds the subsequent stages with successive data collection and systematization. The empirical study [19] adopted a combination of methods and unfolded in three stages:

1) *Study of multiple cases of participatory projects and apps:* which allowed the identification of relevant interface and visualization models for the platform, as well as their systematization through the creation of mood boards and taxonomies for the analysis and design of participatory projects;
2) *Semi-functional prototyping of a mobile application:* which allowed understanding the dynamics of a digital community around visual records of musical events, to obtain opinions on motivations and preferences of a young target audience regarding locative content sharing;
3) *Interviews with experts:* which allowed assessing the receptivity to the platform's concept by experts and cultural institutions that promote events, leading to the identification of relevant contexts of application, as well as strategies, opportunities, and challenges that were paramount for the design of the model.

2.1 Phase 1: Study of Multiple Cases

The main objective of the multiple case study [20] was to map user interfaces and approaches regarding participation and visualization to understand their potentialities to inform the following phases of the research towards the proposed model. The results of the first phase were systematized in mood boards [21, 22] and an analysis matrix composed of a participation taxonomy and a visualization taxonomy.

For the analysis, two samples were identified: i) artistic and R&D participatory projects that explore the synergy between online and offline approaches, including older but innovative and long-lasting projects that remain timeless references; ii) mobile applications (apps) to identify relevant interfaces that explore the correlated visualization of audiovisual resources.

Sample of Artistic and R&D Projects. The sample consists of 18 cases, originating between 1997 and 2016, identified from documentary research and specialized repositories (MITDocubase[1]; Visual Complexity[2]; LABVIS[3]; and ReThinking Visualization[4]). The selection criteria considered the innovative character for their time and the sustainability in terms of longevity (some projects are still ongoing), as well as the diversity of approaches for social participation based on the sharing of audiovisual resources, online and offline. From the analysis of the sample, some relevant aspects are highlighted:

- The diversity of approaches, from automated content aggregation to social systems that empower users to upload their content;
- The large-scale and long-term (several years or decades) projects involving multi-disciplinary production teams and often the materialization in different digital and analogue formats (e.g., books, exhibitions, workshops, etc.);
- The importance of clarifying how people can participate (providing a guiding concept or onboarding instructions in the digital platform) for fostering participation and editorial coherence;
- The flexibility to adapt the initial purpose of the project by being open to shared governance based on partnerships to ensure the sustainability and continuity of the project;
- Preventing technological obsolescence and encouraging an ongoing documenting practice, because in collaborative projects the process is often more important than the results.

Sample of Mobile Apps. To complement the sample of participatory projects, 12 mobile apps were analyzed and organized into four thematic typologies highlighting some features:

- Multimedia notes (quick recording of testimonials; tagging notes with moods using emojis; defining categories for searching and navigating);
- Timelines (granularity of time scales; space-time interfaces);
- Mapping and photo albums (annotated maps; geolocated search using the camera; media galleries integrated into calendars; automatic albums by themes identified in the pictures; collaborative albums; generating collages and videos);

---

[1] https://docubase.mit.edu/.
[2] http://www.visualcomplexity.com/vc/.
[3] https://labvis.eba.ufrj.br/.
[4] https://rethinkingvis.com/.

- Networks and conceptual maps (tridimensional representations; direct manipulation; augmented reality; haptic and natural interaction).

From the two samples, two systematizations outputs were developed providing insights into the model:

Taxonomies of Participation and Visualization. Through the compilation of attributes collected from the various cases, a comprehensive analytical matrix was built to reflect the diversity of possible approaches when analyzing or developing projects and applications (see Fig. 2). The identification of *Who, When, Why, What* and *How*, led to an operative approach between categories of attributes, to promote the adequacy and synergy between participation and visualization, according to the formats, objectives and contexts of each project.

PARTICIPATION					
WHO		WHEN	WHY	WHAT	HOW
Type of participants / Type of co-creation		Moment of participation	subjects' and content producers' motivations	Type of UGC / User submission	User Interactivity
subject; subject-producer; peer-producer; user-producer; user / viewer; edited (before release); radical (during development); peripheral (after distribution)		before; during; after	selected by the author; algorithmic aggregation; rewards; gamification; common interest; self-representation	user behavior/data; document; photo; video; text testemonial / comment; audio testemonial; video testemonial; selfie / profile photo	navigation; overview and explore; gaming; edit or remix; contribute with content; comment, rate or share

VISUALIZATION			
WHO	WHAT		HOW
Type of system	Focus / Predominant Content		Layout model / Organization model
opened and dynamic; opened but curated; closed and curated	media-centric; people-centric; place-centric; story-centric; time-centric; audio or music; captions and headlines; comments and annotations; graphics / maps; photos; videos or animations; 3D or multilayered; annotated map		menus and widgets; network; grid or mosaic; slideshow or playlist; tag cloud; text and image based; video / image based; categories / collections; time and flows; mapping; media navigation; hierarchy and networks; space-time

Fig. 2. Taxonomies of Participation and Visualization.

As an analysis device, we consider that the matrix of taxonomies allows, through cross-categorization, a better understanding of the relationships between the options adopted by authors and made available to users. The taxonomies were adapted from concepts in the domains of Participatory Culture [1, 5], Narrative Visualization [3, 23], Interactive Documentary (iDoc) [24, 25], and Information Design [26, 27].

Mood Boards. By compiling relevant features in user interfaces from the multiple case study, 6 mood boards were categorized: input menus; space-time interfaces; timelines; media galleries; tags and categories; networks and connections (see Fig. 3).

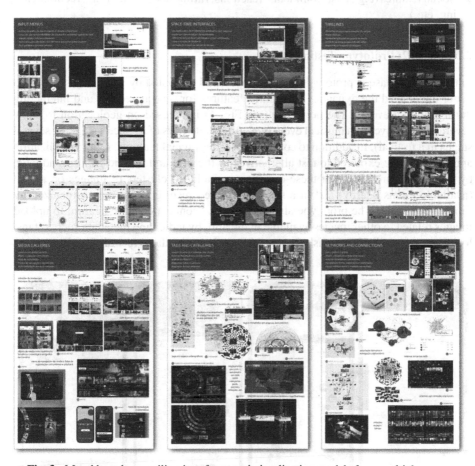

Fig. 3. Mood boards compiling interfaces and visualization models from multiple cases.

These mood boards allowed the graphic systematization of user interfaces and visualization models to assist the prototyping and modelling processes. Accordingly, we highlight some relevant insights emerging from the mood boards:

- Search and filters (e.g., tags; contextual information; relevance and popularity; time and location; etc.);
- Exploratory features (e.g., dashboards; drag-and-drop interfaces; annotation tools; magnification tools);
- Tridimensional navigation (e.g., network diagrams and conceptual maps; virtual and augmented reality, etc.);

- Storytelling (e.g., full-screen visuals; scrollytelling; timelines; story maps; collages; stories and slideshows; collections and galleries; playlists; animations and videos, etc.);
- Social features (e.g., chat; comments; reactions; rating; sharing; inviting; recommending, etc.).

2.2 Phase 2: Prototype Testing

In the second phase, a prototype was developed and evaluated by university students to better understand the dynamics and valued features for sharing records and interacting during cultural events. The prototype (see Fig. 4) is focused on geolocation to show several perspectives of a musical event (e.g., different views of a concert stage, or several stages in a festival). In addition to content upload and social features, some visualization approaches were explored to test alternatives to the grid and mosaic galleries adopted by most platforms. Some of these experiences included clusters of images on a map (available events nearby) and in a timeline (shared records of an event organized by time) (see Fig. 4). The prototype also proposed a "connect content" feature to upload images related to other images available in the app, by indicating metadata such as tags, locations, or people to establish the connections between those records (see Fig. 4).

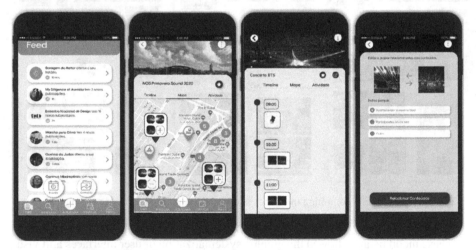

Fig. 4. Prototype interfaces: Feed; Map search; Timeline gallery; Connect content.

In terms of evaluation, the prototype had two iterations of testing with university students. The first assessment was carried out in individual 30-min video call sessions with 10 participants, with a non-functional but navigable version of the prototype, following a script of tasks to evaluate the graphical interface and the features. The participants explored the prototype on their mobile phones and filled in a questionnaire at the end. After corrections to the prototype according to the tests' results, a focus group was held with 5 of the participants to discuss the difficulties and validate the improvements.

Next was implemented the functional version of the prototype with the main functionalities available to simulate the in-loco usage during a real event: create an account; customize the personal profile; search events by location or keyword; subscribe and create events; upload images using the phone camera or files in the device; interact with existing content (react, comment, mark as favorite, browse the timeline of records by temporal clusters). Other advanced features, such as the "connect content", inviting friends or uploading video or audio files were not implemented but were contemplated in the interface. The evaluation was carried out with the 5 users who participated in the focus group. During this evaluation, participants created their profiles and freely used the prototype for one day, reporting their opinions in a final questionnaire. Despite the limitations of the evaluation in terms of time and not being used during a real event due to the COVID-19 pandemic restrictions, the results revealed a unanimous foreseen acceptance of the platform. All provided features were considered useful, although the "connect content" was considered interesting but secondary.

Beyond the technical requirements for the digital platform, we highlight as main contributions to the proposed model the acknowledgement of the importance of providing direct features for sharing content in mobility during events and the importance of activity notifications and statistics regarding uploaded and subscribed content. Also, the customization of the personal profile is essential to the current socializing experience, including, private areas for favorites and content recommendations. Overall, through several features such as notifications, invitations and suggestions from friends, searches by keyword and geographical proximity, the prototype intended to foster social dynamization and discovery of content, thus cherishing collective memories. The motivation for the subject (musical events) was very relevant to the target audience who tested the prototype, as well as the recommendation from friends and strategies of gamification to encourage participation and bring event promoters closer to their audiences. These community aspects were identified as fundamental for the cohesion of a digital platform leveraged from common interests and shared content.

2.3 Phase 3: Interviews with Experts

The last stage of data collection was dedicated to exploratory interviews with experts to present the concept (using a video animation) (see Fig. 1) and to assess the receptivity to a digital platform to collect and visualize collective memories [19]. Through individual 90-min video call semi-structured interviews, conducted with a sample of 11 academics and professionals, some representatives of institutions and reference projects, from the realms of archives, museology, heritage, ethnography, community projects, cultural events, design, participatory media and digital platforms, the aim was to gather insights about relevant use contexts as well as differentiating features and challenges to inform the model and future prototypes.

The interview approach privileged an open conversation about the concept of the digital platform with some structured questions but without restricting the experts' opinions with established decisions about the interface design or features. The transcripts of the interviews were coded using software for qualitative data analysis (QDA) and following the thematic content analysis method [28] to explore the richness of each participant's discourse beyond the topics included in the script. The results [19] were systematized in terms of strategies (for content collection, for evocation and visual elicitation, for visualization models, and for joining and participating) (see Fig. 5), and relevant typologies of use contexts (see Fig. 6).

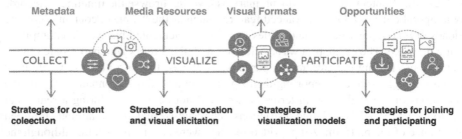

Fig. 5. Parameters and strategies systematized from the experts' interviews.

Fig. 6. Typologies of use contexts systematized from the experts' interviews.

For comparative analysis of the results, the sample was evenly divided into two panels, with one participant sharing both profiles: the panel Culture and Communities (CC) with experts oriented towards humanistic and social sciences domains in the context of cultural and community dynamics; and the panel Platforms and Participation (PP) with experts in the fields of design, digital media, and participatory culture. There was a difference between panels in terms of receptivity and opinions regarding the proposed concept for a digital platform. Namely, the CC panel was more enthusiastic about this mediation tool to facilitate the collection of testimonials in loco and for supporting community activities and events, while the PP panel was more skeptical about people's adoption of another digital platform given the existing competitors, thus, suggesting specialized niches with already motivated target audiences who would be more willing to join and feed this new platform.

3 The MNEMOSCOPE Model

In a broad sense, the modelling process involves a theoretical operationalization to guide prototyping and knowledge transfer, with the flexibility to allow adaptation to different contexts [29]. This investigation, aimed to identify and streamline participation mechanisms to clarify the relevance of the participants' contributions to a collective interest, through visualizations within an iterative dynamic of knowledge discovery and co-creation [30], carried out together with people through digital and face-to-face mediation dynamics [7, 31]. Thus, the physical experience of events reflects on the remembrance mechanism of the digital platform, which also intends to enhance the face-to-face experiences as an expanded hybrid reality based on a permanent process of content activation using mediation strategies.

The technology-mediated model MNEMOSCOPE aims to represent multiple points of view on collective memories of experiences in their observable and sharable dimensions using a participatory platform. Hence, it works, not as a search engine or repository based on taxonomic inventory but, as a storytelling system and a trigger of remembrance. Based on a cyclical and non-sequential collaborative process (see Fig. 7), the digital platform underlying the model aims to explore and discover content through association and derivation. Additionally, stimulated by correlated visualizations of shared records, the model combines a cognitive dimension of content enrichment with an emotional dimension based on the community feeling of belonging to encourage participation. Figure 7 systematizes the model elements, which materialize a hybrid experience, resulting from the synergy between the physical instance (the places where events and experiences occur) and the digital instance (the technological mediation of the platform), taking advantage of georeferencing and locative dynamics during face-to-face participation. Thus, the model depends on three operative components:

- Multimedia Records (content): the *documental layer* of resources evocative of experiences shared by the various participants, consisting of a structured database of the records and their metadata which allow correlated forms of presentation.
- Collective Memories (visualizations): the *aggregation and correlation layer* automatically organizes the records based on defined filters and semantic connections. The resulting visualizations are dynamic and customizable, working as triggers for remembrance and content discovery.
- Digital Community (users): the *social and emotional layer* that feeds the system through social engagement and content sharing. This digital community includes different types of users whose motivation and level of participation is variable (from institutions and event promoters that disseminate content and foster its activation through mediation activities, to more passive and contemplative users, as opposed to others who are more active in contributing with their records).

The participatory platform is the central element of the model, whose digital mediation enables the visualization and co-creation of collective memories, based on shared records. This social dynamic of content sharing and enrichment leads to the constitution of *digital archives* and the consolidation of *online communities*, around common interests, and experiences, with the possibility of replication and adaptation to different contexts. The identified use contexts are cultural content, places, or events dynamized by communities, local organizations, or municipality facilities such as museums, archives, libraries, natural parks, etc.

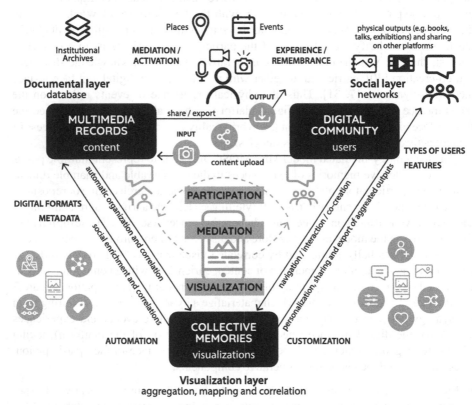

Fig. 7. MNEMOSCOPE model for digital co-creation and visualization of collective memories based on a participatory platform.

The model's components articulate according to three platform principles (Fig. 7) which are mutually interdependent – mediation, visualization, and participation. The visualization and participation mechanisms only exist due to the mediation mechanisms provided by the digital platform, and this mediation is focused on the operationalization of the other two mechanisms. Likewise, visualization mechanisms are inapplicable if they are not activated by participation mechanisms that feed the system with records and through social dynamics that enrich and contextualize it. The three principles unfold into detailed guidelines (Fig. 7), providing good practices for the sustainability of digitally mediated participatory projects and the development of prototypes applied to specific contexts.

Mediation Principle and Guidelines. *The platform should support activities that encourage remembrance and social dynamics around the digital archive of records of experiences shared by various users, with the aim to better represent these collective memories and consolidate the community around them.*

1. Provide **autonomy** to participants, namely through platform **onboarding guidance** complemented by face-to-face **training** actions if necessary;
2. Contemplate **activation and dynamization** activities, through calls to action, challenges and gamification strategies to encourage participation (e.g., sharing new content and content discovery);
3. Explore the **hybrid experience** of **synergy between face-to-face and digital activities**, with individual and group dynamics (e.g., using public interactive displays to allow group access, as well as complementary activities using platform resources, such as printed publications, exhibitions, screenings, talks, etc.);
4. Promote **transparency** regarding the platforms' operating mechanisms and provide **open access** to its contents, to encourage cooperation in future developments and to clarify the usage and safeguard **data privacy** and **intellectual property** policies;
5. Establish and apply **standards of ethical usage and respect for participants' contributions**, which may include more specific rules of use depending on the contexts and the event promoters, namely institutions.

Visualization Principle and Guidelines. *The platform should offer automatic and customizable ways of aggregating, organizing, and presenting shared resources, with the aim of enhancing their critical and creative exploration from multiple perspectives.*

1. Records should use **formats** that best allow the user to **document, narrate, and evoke the emotion of their experience**, with the potential to instigate identification and empathy in other participants;
2. Some **metadata may be automatically extracted** from the digital file (e.g., timestamp, georeferencing, capture parameters, etc.), as well as through computer vision APIs to obtain semantic classification labels, although it is always advisable that the user verify them;
3. The **contextual information provided by users**, complementary to the automatically extracted metadata, should focus on the descriptive and emotional dimension of the records, to highlight their symbolic and evocative importance to collective memory;
4. The contextual information should adopt **metadata standards** (e.g., Dublin Core; Linked Open Data; IIIF Framework, etc.), which aim for **interoperability** with other databases to allow possible integrations;
5. The **automatic aggregation/organization** mechanism should adopt relevance and metadata criteria (e.g., location, date, description, users, keywords, etc.) to allow filtering and generating correlated visualizations;
6. The platform should provide different **interactive visualization models** (non-linear), allowing **macro and micro content navigation and discovery** from different perspectives (e.g., time-based, place-based, users-based, etc.), and may focus on semantic parameters (e.g., categories, keywords, etc.);
7. The platform should **generate curated presentation formats** (linear) as '**memory capsules**', according to defined criteria namely themes and social engagement around

the records (e.g., popularity, user interaction, comments and tagging, etc.), which may be **customized and shared** by users inside and outside the platform (e.g., collages, stories, animations, videos, etc.);

8. The platform may allow **exporting formats and statistics** to enable research (studies about shared content, social dynamics, and co-created storytelling) and give back to the communities through activities and physical formats such as publications, exhibitions, public screenings, etc.

Participation Principle and Guidelines. *The platform should provide functional features for contribution, exploration, interaction, and creation, with the aim of enhancing social dynamics of enrichment, recombination, and co-creation, based on the content shared by multiple users.*

1. The platform may adopt open or semi-opened participation reflected on the permissions assigned to different **user roles** (e.g., the distinction between follower/participant permissions and the event promoters who have an administration role, including mediation and content validation, although a peer review/report system is advisable);

2. Considering **levels of motivation for participation** (e.g., from *prosumers* who are active content creators to *lurkers* who are more passive spectators) users' **badges** can be adopted to encourage and reward participation by highlighting users who stand out in terms of engagement, starting conversation threads, sharing content, creating visual narratives, etc.;

3. The platform should provide a **user profile area** including personal information and activity **notifications** regarding the events created and followed by the user (e.g., shared content, social engagement, bookmarked content and customized formats);

4. The **content input feature** should allow the mobile sharing of records using mobile devices' camera or the device storage, namely image, video and audio files and may also include computer vision-API and speech-to-text features to enrich content metadata;

5. The **exploration features** should provide semantic filters and interactive viewing modes for content discovery and navigation through different areas of the platform (e.g., personal profile, interactive views, thematic collections and automatic or user-customized 'memory capsules' that can be saved and shared outside the platform);

6. The **interaction features** to allow social dynamics around content shared by users (e.g., reaction, comments, bookmarks, tagging people, connecting related content, etc.) to enrich it and refine the aggregation and recommendation system;

7. The **personalization features** for content curation and co-creation using the resources shared by users and the automatically generated outputs (e.g., thematic collections, collages, stories, animations, videos, etc.) to foster co-creation and visual storytelling.

Conceptually, the model was designed in a flexible way to be able to contemplate two approaches: i) to be one broad scope platform, in which several 'memory projects' can be created and assigned to different themes/events with targeted audiences; ii) to allow the creation of different platforms for specific projects/events, designed from scratch to address specialized needs and purposes, based on the principles underlying the model. Such adaptations to niche contexts and uses are welcome, as they may contribute to improving and expanding the model, as an increment, extension, or derivation, from a perspective of open access to knowledge and scientific cooperation.

4 Final Considerations and Future Work

The article describes the research process using different methods and instruments (study of multiple cases; prototyping; and interviews with experts) to design a technology-mediated model for co-creation and visualization of collective memories. The model is directed by principles and guidelines of mediation, visualization, and participation, and based on a digital platform which constitutes simultaneously a collaborative archive and a digital community around records of shared events and experiences. Compared to other participatory projects and platforms (including social media), the differentiating aspect is the visual and semantic correlation of multimedia records to be socially enriched, instigated by visualizations that depict different points of view and exploratory possibilities.

In this regard, the core of the digital platform stands out as an instrument of storytelling based on the sharing of visual records and testimonies, namely mobile captures during events and their real-time integration in a structured database. Some contexts of use involving communities and shared experiences identified during the study include cultural events like concerts, exhibitions, cultural intangible heritage and traditional celebrations, as well as oral testimonials, and life stories. The model's versatility also contemplates its application for research purposes regarding visual studies, participatory culture studies and contemporary social archiving practices, as a complementary tool for documenting and analyzing participation dynamics and shared multimedia content.

Despite the limitations of the empirical study, namely not being able to test a functional prototype during real events due to the COVID-19 pandemic restrictions, some future challenges for the implementation of the platform were also identified to help anticipate and overcome upcoming difficulties. Some of the identified challenges are: i) the users' cost of adoption due to the competition of other digital platforms and social media; ii) the compromising of sustainability because of being too dependent on user participation and resources; iii) the conditioned access to quality resources and copyright issues regarding automatic aggregation; iv) promoting disinformation due to poorly contextualized resources; v) discourage participation and personal stories by being too technical or specialized; vi) and trigger possible conflicts around sensitive topics because collective memory is not consensual. On the other hand, opportunities were also identified: i) the need to aggregate and correlate disperse information, namely regarding several typologies of cultural heritage; ii) valuing the storytelling dimension related to personal stories making easy-to-capture testimonials in mobility; iii) and enhancing the experience of events by giving voice to the several agents involved including the audiences and documenting invisible aspects from planning, preparation and backstage, to in loco records and post-event content sharing and remembering.

The potential that emerged from this research, which culminated in the model, was translated into an R&D project approved for funding. The POLARISCOPE project was initiated in February 2023 and will run over a period of three years, focused on the implementation and user testing of a functional platform in field trials during cultural events and experiences in Portugal. The casual and institutional usages of the platform in different territories and events will allow the co-creation and transfer of innovation and knowledge to the community, to support meaningful participation and instigate critical debate and creativity around collective memories.

Acknowledgements. The research is funded by FCT - Fundação para a Ciência e a Tecnologia (Grant nr. SFRH/BD/132780/2017). The authors acknowledge the collaboration of University of Aveiro students who participated in the prototyping process and the user evaluation, and the interviewed experts. This work contributed to the preliminary research for the R&D project POLARISCOPE (grant agreement no. 2022.04424.PTDC) also funded by FCT.

References

1. Jenkins, H.: Convergence Culture: Where Old and New Media Collide. University Press, New York (2008)
2. Alexander, B.: The New Digital Storytelling - Creating Narratives with New Media. Praeger, Santa Barbara, California (2011)
3. Segel, E., Heer, J.: Narrative visualization: telling stories with data. Vis. Comput. Graph. IEEE Trans. **16**(6), 1139–1148 (2010)
4. Shneiderman, B.: The eyes have it: a task by data type taxonomy for information visualizations. In: Proceedings of the 1996 IEEE Symposium on Visual Languages (VL '96), pp. 336–343. IEEE Computer Society (1996)
5. Manovich, L.: The Language of New Media. The MIT Press, Cambridge, Massachusetts (2001)
6. Cairo, A.: The Functional Art – an Introduction to Information Graphics and Visualization. New Riders, USA (2013)
7. Huybrechts, L. (ed.): Participation is Risky – Approaches to Joint Creative Processes. Valiz, Amsterdam (2014)
8. Drucker, J.: Graphesis: Visual knowledge production and representation (2011)
9. Dijck, J.V.: Mediated Memories in the Digital Age. Stanford University Press, Stanford (2007)
10. Ernst, W.: Digital Memory and the Archive. University of Minnesota Press, Minneapolis, London (2013)
11. Levenberg, I., Neilson, T., Rheams, D.: Research Methods for the Digital Humanities. Palgrave Macmillan (2018)
12. Manovich, L.: Cultural Analytics. The MIT Press, Cambridge, London (2020)
13. Pousman, Z., Stasko, J., Mateas, M.: Casual information visualization: depictions of data in everyday life. Vis. Comput. Graph. IEEE Trans. **13**(6), 1145–1152 (2007)
14. Whitelaw, M.: Generous interfaces for digital cultural collections. Digit. Hum. Q. **9**(1) (2015)
15. Surowiecki, J.: The Wisdom of Crowds: Why the Many are Smarter than the Few and How Collective Wisdom Shapes Business, Economies, Societies, and Nations. Doubleday, New York (2004)
16. Brabham, D.C.: Crowdsourcing. The MIT Press, Cambridge, London (2013)
17. Velhinho, A.: Sobre a Influência da Visualização e da Participação na Cultura Visual em Rede do Século XXI e na Cocriação Digital de Memórias Coletivas [Doctoral thesis]. Faculdade de Belas-Artes da Universidade de Lisboa (2023)
18. Glaser, B.G., Strauss, A.L.: The Discovery of Grounded Theory - Strategies for Qualitative Research. Routledge, London, New York (2017)

19. Velhinho, A., Almeida, P.: Sharing and visualizing collective memories – contexts and strategies for a participatory platform. In: Abásolo, M., Abreu, J., Almeida, P., Silva, T. (eds.) Communications in Computer and Information Science, pp. 3–14. Springer International Publishing (2020). https://doi.org/10.1007/978-3-030-81996-5_1
20. Yin, R.K.: Case Study Research – Design and Methods. Sage Publications, EUA (1994)
21. Federizzi, C.L., Halpern, M.C., Machado, T.L., Gerenda, F.: O moodboard como ferramenta metaprojetual: um estudo sobre o caso Smart! In: 11º Congresso Brasileiro de Pesquisa e Desenvolvimento em Design, Blucher Design Proceedings, vol. 1, 2014, pp. 1101–1112 (2014)
22. Koch, J., Taffin, N., Lucero, A., Mackay, W.E.: SemanticCollage: enriching digital mood board design with semantic labels. In: DIS '20: Proceedings of the 2020 ACM Designing Interactive Systems Conference, pp. 407–418 (2020)
23. Figueiras, A.: How to tell stories using visualization: strategies towards Narrative Visualization [Doctoral thesis]. Faculdade de Ciências Sociais e Humanas da Universidade Nova de Lisboa (2016)
24. Gaudenzi, S.: The Living Documentary: from representing reality to co-creating reality in digital interactive documentary [Doctoral thesis]. University of London (2013)
25. Weight, J.: At the edge of documentary: participatory online nonfiction. In: TEXT, 17(Special Issue 18), 1–14 Nonfiction Now (2013)
26. Lima, M.: Visual Complexity. Mapping Patterns of Information. Princeton Architectural Press, New York (2011)
27. Meirelles, I.: Design for Information. An introduction to the histories, theories, and best practices behind effective information visualizations. Rockport Publishers, Gloucester, Massachusetts (2013)
28. Bardin L.: Análise de Conteúdo. Edições 70, Almedina Brasil, São Paulo (2011)
29. Silva, A.M.: Modelos e Modelizações em Ciência da Informação: O Modelo eLit.pt e a investigação em literacia informacional. In: Prisma.com (Portugal), no. 13, pp. 298–353 (2010)
30. Sampaio, C.P., Martins, S.B.: Projetos de pesquisa e desenvolvimento em design, sustentabilidade e inovação: bases teóricas para a contribuição do design. In: Design, Artefatos e Sistema Sustentável, pp. 35–58, (2018)
31. Sousa, F.: The Participation in the Safeguarding of the Intangible Cultural Heritage. The role of Communities, Groups and Individuals. Memória Imaterial CRL, Alenquer (2018)

Dynamic Configuration of Panoramic Virtual Tours

Carlos Alberto Flores Sanjurjo, Joaquín Danilo Pina Amargós(✉) ⓘ,
and Ariel Alfonso Fernández Santana

Universidad Tecnológica de La Habana "José Antonio Echeverría" (CUJAE),
Havana, Cuba
jpina@ceis.cujae.edu.cu

Abstract. Virtual tours allow for the simulation of human presence in specific locations from the comfort of one's home through immersive experiences. Currently, they are widely used by individuals and even large companies. There are multiple software applications that enable the creation of these tours, but most of them only allow for the visualization of static scenes that cannot be modified. Moreover, these software applications are proprietary, which means they cannot be improved or have new functionalities added, and their use is prohibited in certain countries due to unilateral sanctions imposed by foreign powers. To address this problem, research was conducted to identify a technology that would enable the development of software providing Cuba with technological independence while meeting the necessary requirements. Based on this, it was decided to utilize open-source technologies associated with JavaScript, employing Node, Nest.js, and Mongo DB for the backend to handle data persistence. For the visual functionalities associated with virtual reality, Three.js, a powerful open-source JavaScript library with a wide range of available functions, was chosen. As the solution demands minimal resources, the results can be applied to interactive digital television in low-performance smart set-top boxes, thereby extending their use in education and cultural contexts. This work contributes to the development of different sectors of society and promotes the growth of technological sovereignty in countries.

Keywords: virtual reality · virtual tour · free software

1 Introduction

Since the emergence of computer science, humans have dreamed of the possibility of immersing themselves in alternative worlds created virtually, to experience sensations that they could not feel in real life. Virtual reality encloses a sphere of knowledge that is responsible for the representation of scenes, multimedia and objects, with a close relationship with each other, to form a real experience. Several authors define virtual reality as the presence of the human in the space

M. J. Abásolo et al. (Eds.): jAUTI 2022, CCIS 1820, pp. 36–50, 2023.
https://doi.org/10.1007/978-3-031-45611-4_3

generated by the computer in an interactive way, where the user comes into contact with the computer with a practically legitimate world [9].

Nowadays, the presence of virtual reality is something common. For example, it can be found in architectural designs, in video games, in aircraft and automobile simulators, in shooting simulators, in advertisements made by advertising companies and in the education, art and entertainment sectors [7]. Its applications can also be found in medicine such as in minimally accessible surgical procedures, in anatomy and in rehabilitation [5].

One of the ways to represent an environment through virtual reality are virtual tours, a method of representing reality that has become very popular in recent years [10]. They are used in the real estate branch to promote their products without the need for the physical presence of customers since they can be spread through the internet [4]. They are also used in the educational and artistic field through the representation of museums and centers of interest, to enhance the cultural heritage of the nation. In addition, in criminology they provide the ability to reconstruct a crime scene to clarify the events [4].

There are applications for the creation of virtual tours, which interactively represent a certain place through panoramic images or 3D models [11]. In addition, they allow the interaction of users with the environment to navigate between scenes or visualize certain points of interest. Another of the features they have is navigation through an automatic route through the location [10]. These tools provide the ability to incorporate audio, images, videos, texts and directions into the tours. With the aim of representing a more real virtual world, virtual tours use three fundamental aspects of virtual reality: immersion, real time and interaction [3].

Currently, the web is the most used medium by users through any device that has the ability to connect to the internet, achieving access to anywhere in the world in a matter of seconds. In it we can find all kinds of information that allows overcoming and, in addition, facilitates the realization of any type of research. For these reasons, innovative technologies have emerged to improve users' experiences on the web every day.

The benefits of this work will be reflected in the economic field, its application in tourism will allow the country's hotels to be promoted, which can result in a greater number of customers, constituting a greater source of income. In addition, with its realization, technological sovereignty will be acquired, so using the free software that addresses the research, applications similar to these can be developed, without depending on third parties, and, above all, without buying in the international market. The frequent use of virtual tours in the country will be beneficial to enhance the cultural and historical heritage of the nation, promoting historical places, museums, art galleries, tourist centers, wild areas, among others. They also constitute a way to encourage the education of young people, bringing them closer to the history of Cuba in a visual, modern and attractive way.

In this paper, the development of a system that allows the visualization and dynamic shaping of virtual tours with panoramic views is exposed, using technologies based on free software in a web environment. Next, the antecedents found in the specialized literature are addressed and a foundation of the chosen technological selection is made. Then the proposed solution is exposed to demonstrate the feasibility of dynamic shaping and visualization of virtual tours on the web, using free technology, through a functional prototype. Finally, the results achieved with the present research are presented and discussed.

2   Previous Works and Technological Selection

A study of multiple free applications that could meet the parameters addressed in this research was carried out. They are shown below along with their main limitations:

1. Marzipano [1]
   - Does not allow the persistence of data of virtual tours.
   - It is only compatible with Firefox and Chrome browsers.
   - Does not allow the use of multimedia uploaded from the web.
2. Pano2VR [2]
   - It has a free demo with very few features.
   - To access all its features, a paid license must be purchased.

Therefore, free applications do not have all the necessary functionalities for the development and visualization of interactive virtual tours, nor do they allow their dynamic configuration. On the other hand, other applications provide a greater amount of functionality but are not accessible to Cuba or are proprietary.

The research proposes a method of dynamic construction for tours where the behavior of all the points of interest in it can be modified. To prevent the client application from overloading, all data and multimedia will be stored on a web server that will be accessed through the network. This in turn will allow any user to add or modify information in the same application and it will be updated automatically.

Taking into account the above background, this paper proposes the adoption of open technologies and standards in Interactive Digital Television for education and entertainment.

It is desired that the system be accessible from different devices, so it was decided to develop it in a web environment, thus allowing its visualization using a browser from both a computer and a mobile device or tablet. The above allows its application on any device that is configured to work as a second screen on interactive digital television [6].

To illustrate the technological selection made, the Table 1 is presented where a comparison of the web 360 technologies referred to above in the background of the research is shown.

Table 1. Web 360 technologies

Attribute	A-frame	Pannellum	Marzipano.js	Three.js
License	MIT	MIT	MIT	MIT
Learning curve	High	Medium	Low	Medium
Documentation	Medium	Medium	Medium	High
Latest Stable Version	February/2021	November/2019	November/2021	April/2022

After performing the previous analysis it was decided to use *Three.js* for the management of virtual reality on the client side. The criteria on which this decision was based are presented below:

1. It presents *MIT* license so it can be used freely.
2. Despite having an average learning curve, the authors had already worked with this library before, so they were very familiar with it.
3. It presents a lot of documentation, tutorials and guides for developing applications.
4. The latest stable version was recently released in April 2022.

Table 2 shows a comparison of the technologies for client-side development referred to in the previous heading.

Table 2. Frontend technologies

Attribute	Angular.JS	VueJS	React.js
DOM	Regular	Virtual	Virtual
Learning curve	High	Low	Low
Packaging	Weak	Strong	Strong
MVC	Present	Inspired	View layer only

After performing the above analysis it was decided to use *React.js* for client-side development. The criteria on which this decision was based are presented below:

1. It uses a virtual *DOM* that allows a great performance.
2. It has a low learning curve and uses to a great extent the functionalities of *JavaScript*.
3. It does not use the *MVC* pattern, however, given the architecture to be used that will be discussed in the next section, this does not represent a disadvantage.

The Table 3 shows a comparison of the *frameworks* for server-side development referred to above.

Table 3. Backend technologies

Attribute	Asp.Net	Spring	NestJS
Architecture	Yes	Yes	Yes
Resource requirements	High	High	Low
Amount of code	Medium	High	Low
Programming language	C Sharp	Java	JavaScript

After performing the above analysis it was decided to use *NestJS* for the development of the application on the server side. The criteria on which this decision was based are presented below:

1. It provides a default architecture.
2. The factor that most influenced the choice is that it consumes very few system resources.
3. It allows to develop applications using a small amount of code, which facilitates testing.
4. It uses the programming language *JavaScript*, which implies that the entire system can be realized in a single language.

3   Proposed Solution

In this work it is necessary to demonstrate through a functional prototype the feasibility of the dynamic conformation and visualization of virtual tours on the web using free technology. It should include the possibility of interacting with the environment, navigating between scenes, displaying images and displaying information about elements of interest present in the scene.

Since no clearly defined process was identified in the business modeling, a description of the entities and relationships involved in it was considered. For this reason, there is no business use case diagram and the decision was made to use a domain model for the representation. The Fig. 1 shows the graphical representation of the system domain together with a glossary of terms in the Table 4 for a better understanding of the system.

The functional requirements of the system are shown in the Table 5.

As can be seen in the Table 6 one of the quality requirements of the system is availability. To ensure compliance with this requirement, it was decided to develop the application using a microservices-based architecture.

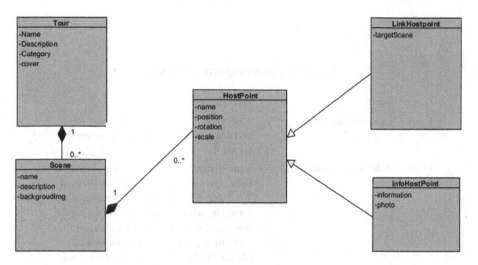

Fig. 1. Domain model.

Table 4. Definition of main entities and concepts

Entity	Description
Tour	It represents a virtual tour project, it has the set of scenes that make up the entire tour.
Scene	It represents a scene, it is the set of all the different types of elements that make up the virtual tour.
LinkHostpoint	It is represented as a sphere component in Three.js and allows scrolling between the scenes of the tour.
InfoHostpoint	It is represented as a sphere component in Three.js and allows to display a certain information to the user

Microservices refers to a service-oriented architecture that seeks to decompose an application into different services, with the aim of obtaining high availability, low coupling, decentralization and fault tolerance. It is an ideal architecture for high traffic and high availability scenarios.

Table 5. Functional requirements.

Code	Name	Description
C-01	View virtual tours	The visitor is able to visualize the virtual tours that he has previously created.
C-02	Make up virtual tour	The editor is able to create a virtual tour, by tapping the Create Virtual Tour button, you will be shown a form, in which you must write name, description, category of the tour and, in addition, you must select a photo for the cover of the tour and thus start creating the tour.
C-03	Load the scene	When the user accesses a virtual tour, the system automatically loads the scenes associated with this tour.
C-04	Load *infoHostPots*	When accessing a scene the system automatically loads the *infoHotsPots* associated with the current scene.
C-05	Load *linkHostPots*	When accessing a scene the system automatically loads the *linkHotsPots* associated with the current scene.
C-06	Managing the scene	The editor is able to create, edit and delete the scenes within the virtual tour, by clicking on the respective buttons for each action.
C-07	Managing *linkHostPots*	The editor is able to create, edit and delete the *linkHostPots* within the scene by clicking on the respective buttons to each action.
C-08	Managing *infoHostPots*	The editor is able to create, edit and delete the *infoHostPots* within the scene by clicking on the respective buttons to each action.
C-9	Registering user	To access the system all users must register in advance.
C-10	Authenticate *linkHostPot*	To access the system the user must provide a username and password that were previously registered

Table 6. Quality requirements

Code	Name	Description
C-01	Usability	A simple and intuitive interface should be guaranteed.
C-02	Navigability	Legible and easy-to-remember URLs should be guaranteed, as well as being able to navigate between pages without using the browser options.
C-03	Fault tolerance	It should be ensured that errors and unexpected events do not involve the collapse of the entire system.
C-04	High availability	System operation must be guaranteed at all times of the day

The Fig. 2 shows the system use case diagram which contains the functionalities to be implemented that the system should provide.

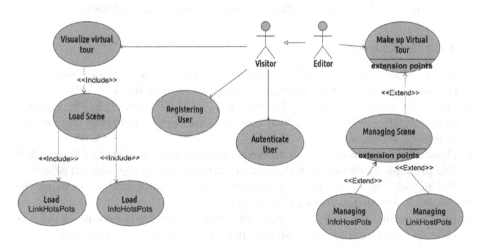

Fig. 2. System use case diagram.

For the implementation of this architecture in this solution, a design strategy based on business core was followed. This means that each entity identified in the domain model represents a microservice, as can be seen in the folder structure shown in the Fig. 3.

Fig. 3. Folder structure of the *backend*.

Each microservice can be built in a different language, which facilitates teamwork. The following section demonstrates compliance with the design patterns that guarantee a better quality in the construction of this architecture.

Principles of Design

1. *Open – Close*: This principle is evident in most of the solution, because all the design patterns of the previous proposal comply with it.
2. *Once and Only Once Rule*: This principle can be evidenced in the creation of the *InfoHostpots*, a procedure that is implemented following the pattern *Template Methods*.
3. Design towards interfaces, not towards implementations: Like the *Open-Close* this principle is evident in all the design patterns used in the solution proposal.
4. *Hollywood*: This is one of the principles that are manifested when using the *Template Methods* pattern in the solution.
5. Encapsulating variability: A principle that is demonstrated by using the *Observer* pattern and the *Prototype* pattern in the solution proposal.
6. Law of *Deméter*: Like the previous principle, its fulfillment is manifested in the use of the patterns *Observer* and *Prototype*.
7. Low coupling: Likewise, it is another of the principles that are evidenced by having used the *Observer* and *Prototype* patterns in the proposed solution.

To fulfill the objective of this research, it was decided to deploy the application in a web environment. Which is aimed at users who access a web server where the virtual tour client will be hosted through a browser, this in turn, will communicate with the servers where the different microservices of the *backend* and their respective databases will be hosted through the *HTTP* protocol.

The Fig. 4 shows the deployment diagram of the system as a web application based on microservices.

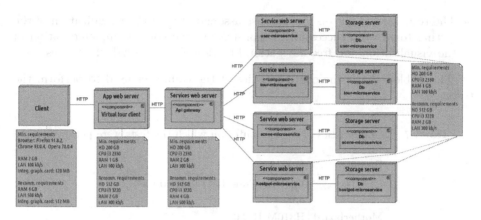

Fig. 4. Deployment diagram.

The feasibility of the dynamic configuration of interactive virtual tours in free development environments is irrefutable, both practical, theoretical and methodological. By demonstrating that they have the means to achieve this, they would be gaining technological independence, offering an option that would otherwise be very expensive.

According to [4,8] the use of virtual tours as a learning method motivates students, in addition, to demonstrate that the knowledge that is consolidated is greater. It should also be taken into account that the digitization of the nation's heritage is important and virtual tours to museums, monuments and the like contribute to preserving it by making it accessible to a wider audience in a more attractive and modern way.

Based on the above, it is considered that the realization of this work is feasible, because the selected technologies allow to fulfill the general objective set. The basic needs would be to have a set of panoramic images and a device that allows the execution of a web browser to access the application. The minimum and recommended customer requirements prove that even low-performance devices can display the virtual tour. The above allows its application on any device that is configured to work as a second screen on interactive digital television.

4 Analysis of the Results

Once the testing process is completed, the results obtained are analyzed:

- The designed prototype covered all the functional requirements and was a key element for the execution of the test cases.
- The tests associated with the use cases related to the processing of the interactions of the *infoHostpot* and *linkHostpot* yielded successful results. This shows a correct implementation of the interaction functionalities in the virtual tour.
- The tests associated with the use cases related to the creation of the virtual tours and their components, showed that the dynamic conformation of the virtual tours is fulfilled.

- The tests carried out on the use case associated with the visualization of the virtual tours were successful, demonstrating the correct implementation of the visualization and free navigation functionalities through the scenes.

The Table 7 shows the characteristics of the computer used to perform the tests.

Table 7. Characteristics of the computer on which the tests were performed

Resource	Features
CPU	Intel(R) Core(TM) i3-8100 CPU 3.60 GHz
Motherboard	H310M H 2.0
GPU	Intel UHD Graphics 630
RAM	4 GB DDR4 1200 MHz
HDD	1 TB

Workflow. When starting to work with the system the user must authenticate, after this, all the virtual tours that the user has created are displayed on the screen. At this point you can choose whether to create a new virtual tour or access one that has been previously created. The above can be seen in the Fig. 5.

Fig. 5. Screenshot *List of virtual tour.*

When accessing *Edit tour*, the screen that will allow the user to make up the tour is displayed. It is necessary to familiarize yourself with this view before starting to edit the route. In the window shown in Fig. 6 and in Fig. 7 it can be seen that:

- In the bottom bar you will find all the created scenes.
- In the left sidebar there is an inspector that dynamically displays the data of the components that intervene in the scene.
- On the top bar there is a *Elements* button that allows the creation of the points of interest in the scene.
- On the rest of the screen is the scene with its corresponding panoramic image.
- A window appears on the screen with the form to create a scene by pressing the add button.

Fig. 6. Application screenshot *Virtual tour Editor*, main functionalities are shown (The texts are displayed in Spanish).

As you can see the user is able to create a virtual tour without coding. These tours can be personalized using any panoramic photo that is desired. In addition, the inclusion of information points allows an interactive experience, because the information that the user wants can be incorporated into them. In the same way, by adding the transition points, the ability to make a tour of several scenes within the same tour is made possible.

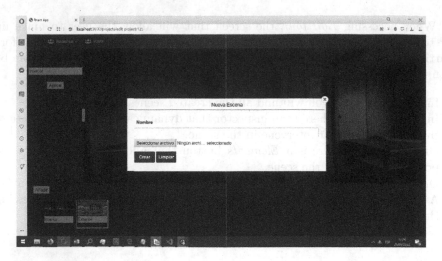

Fig. 7. Application screenshot *Virtual tour Editor*, functionality *Add scene* (The texts are displayed in Spanish).

After the dynamic configuration of the tour is completed, the user is able to visualize it by clicking on the visualize button that is located on the *List of Virtual tours* screen. This view promotes a partial immersion in the route, allowing the user to interact with the elements of the environment created previously. This approach can be seen in the Fig. 8.

Fig. 8. Application screenshot *Visualization of virtual tour*. The content appears in Spanish.

5   Conclusions

By carrying out this research, the objectives set were fulfilled arriving at the following conclusions: The study of the state of the art demonstrated the need to have a system capable of shaping and visualizing a virtual tour, as well as interacting with elements within it. Virtual tours have a wide use, standing out in marketing and the tourism industry, in addition, they are a good means of learning and contribute to preserving and enhancing the cultural and historical heritage of the nation. The main features that a 360 virtual tour should have are: navigating freely between scenes and displaying information about points of interest in the form of text and multimedia elements. The development of interactive 360 virtual tours based on JavaScript technologies in a free environment is feasible, offering technological sovereignty to the country. It was possible to develop the dynamic configuration of the virtual tour by allowing the modification of all its components without modifying the code. The use of the tests with black box approach allowed to verify that the functionalities that demonstrate the visualization and dynamic conformation were fulfilled satisfactorily, guaranteeing the quality of the product. The implemented system satisfies the problem posed at the beginning of the work in a free development environment. The minimum and recommended client requirements demostrate that even low-performance devices like second screen on interactive digital television can display the virtual tour.

To give continuity to this work, it is recommended to: Allow exporting each tour created as a *react* project for its incorporation into other web systems. Implement a desktop or mobile application to allow offline work of the system. Allow users to share their tours through the same system or using social networks.

Acknowledgements. This research has been supported by the Pérez-Guerrero Trust Fund for South-South Cooperation (PGTF) of the United Nations Development Program (UNDP) project INT/19/K08 and the Ministry of Science, Technology and Environment of Cuba (CITMA) project NPN223LH006-005 of TVDi.

References

1. https://www.marzipano.net (2014). Accessed 10 May 2022
2. https://ggnome.com/pano2vr (2014). Accessed 10 May 2022
3. Burdea, G.C., Coiffet, P.: Virtual reality technology. Int. J. e-Collab. **2**(1), 61–64 (2006)
4. Chiao, H.M., Chen, Y.L., Huang, W.H.: Examining the usability of an online virtual tour-guiding platform for cultural tourism education. J. Hosp. Leis. Sport Tour. Educ. **23**, 29–38 (2018)
5. Dimbwadyo-Terrer, I.: Realidad virtual en procedimientos quirúrgicos: Nuevos entornos de aplicación. NeuroRehabNews (Octubre) (2017)
6. Guo, M.: Second screening: measuring second screen user behavior in a social television viewing environment. Int. J. Media Manag. **22**(2), 97–116 (2020). https://doi.org/10.1080/14241277.2020.1803326

7. Kim, J.S., Kim, S.J., Park, S.N., Shin, J.W., Kwon, S.Y.: A study on the development of VR-based education and culture program in public libraries. J. Korean Soc. Inf. Manag. **38**(2), 87–112 (2021)
8. Loures Brandão, G.V., Henriques do Amaral, W.D., Rabite de Almeida, C.A., Barroso Castañon, J.A.: Virtual reality as a tool for teaching architecture. In: Marcus, A., Wang, W. (eds.) DUXU 2018. LNCS, vol. 10919, pp. 73–82. Springer, Cham (2018). https://doi.org/10.1007/978-3-319-91803-7_6
9. Mazuryk, T., Gervautz, M.: Virtual reality-history, applications, technology and future (1996)
10. Pincay Bermello, V.R., Rivas Rodríguez, M.J.: Tour virtual interactivo 360 de las instalaciones de la Universidad de Guayaquil. B.S. thesis, Universidad de Guayaquil. Facultad de Ciencias Matemáticas y Físicas ... (2021)
11. Widiyaningtyas, T., Prasetya, D.D., Wibawa, A.P.: Web-based campus virtual tour application using orb image stitching. In: 2018 5th International Conference on Electrical Engineering, Computer Science and Informatics (EECSI), pp. 46–49. IEEE (2018)

Audiovisual Consumption

Personalized Notifications for the TV Ecosystem: Field Trial of an iTV Solution

Ana Velhinho[1]([✉]) [iD], João Encarnação[1] [iD], Simão Bentes[1] [iD], Juliana Camargo[1] [iD], Gabriel Faria[1], Enrickson Varsori[1] [iD], Telmo Silva[1] [iD], and Rita Santos[2] [iD]

[1] Digimedia, Department of Communication and Art, University of Aveiro, 3810-193 Aveiro, Portugal
{ana.velhinho,jrangel29,bentes,julianacamargo,g.martinsfaria, varsori,tsilva}@ua.pt
[2] Digimedia, Águeda School of Technology and Management, University of Aveiro, 3754-909 Aveiro, Portugal
rita.santos@ua.pt

Abstract. In the context of the proliferation of push notifications on several devices, a mechanism of personalized notifications is proposed to the TV ecosystem to assess its potential. After identifying relevant use scenarios through a literature review, with validation through focus groups, a field trial was carried out to test a solution in partnership with a Portuguese IPTV provider. For this purpose, a notifications managing platform was developed to create personalized notifications to users' set-top-boxes (STB). Over different timeframes and STB triggers, several thematic categories of notifications were tested, namely: daily routines with weather forecast; morning and evening news; calendar appointments and local events; health alerts, such as medication intake; suggestion of food delivery services; and reminders that a regular show is staring in 5 min enabling to directly switch the channel. The field trial allowed measuring the acceptance of the solution, regarding schedules and categories, as well as obtaining suggestions for improvements and adding other notifications. The results gathered from delivery rates provided by the notifications platform and a post-trial survey were analyzed and stratified according to different age groups and household compositions, to understand their relevance regarding television as a shared device. Overall, there was a positive response to TV notifications in terms of the usefulness of the messages (85%) and a foreseen interest to use the service in the future (80%), although with the need for fine-tuning sending schedules and allowing the synchronization with mobile devices, to be implemented in upcoming iterations of the prototype.

Keywords: Push notifications · iTV · Field Trial · Notifications manager prototype

1 Introduction

Push notifications constitute a message mechanism that catches users' attention multiple times per day on their devices, thus becoming a prevalent way of accessing information. Statistics for 2023 [1] indicate that people are more receptive to push notifications if

M. J. Abásolo et al. (Eds.): jAUTI 2022, CCIS 1820, pp. 53–67, 2023.
https://doi.org/10.1007/978-3-031-45611-4_4

they can choose from which apps they wish to receive them, with a preference for social media (57,42%) and news and information (45,94%). Other relevant aspects to increase reaction rates are tailored sending times (40%); targeted sending (39%), and advanced personalization (400%).

Complementary to the previous literature review about related work and the potential of TV notifications conducted within this research [2], other studies also highlight the importance of notifications' temporality. Namely, by identifying the moments when people value the most and dedicate more time to information and news messages on mobile devices [3]. In the television context, notifications are a less explored mechanism, because TV continues to be used collectively and may raise some privacy issues [4]. Nevertheless, the proliferation of Smart TVs and Hybrid Broadcast Broadband TVs (HbbTV) reinforced the Smart Home experience [5] and boosted marketing tools based on notifications to generate and measure engagement, related to viewing behaviours towards apps and streaming platforms. Natively, Amazon Fire TV incorporates Amazon Device Messaging (ADM) that generates analytics for measuring engagement but also admits Android Notifications API for sending local notifications outside the app's UI of Fire TV [6]. As for Netflix, it incorporates a Rapid Event Notification System (RENO), which uses a hybrid push-and-pull communication model across various platforms and devices [7].

In this context, this paper presents the results of the field trial of an iTV solution to send notifications to TV set-top boxes (STBs). The paper is divided into five sections: the first section introduces the background and the scope of the study; the second section presents the research project and the system architecture of the proposed solution; the third section details the phases of the methodological approach; the fourth section presents the results of the field trial; and the sixth section closed with an overview of the outcomes of the study and indicates future work.

2 Over TV – Personalized Notifications for the TV Ecosystem

The OverTV project results from a partnership between academia – University of Aveiro – and an IPTV provider – Altice Labs – to develop a solution for personalized notifications towards the TV ecosystem, mediated by a web platform [8] developed to generate, schedule, and monitor several types of messages (see Fig. 1).

The iTV notifications solution (see Fig. 1) comprises the user interface of the platform consisting of a web application and data storage and management. When a page is opened, a request is made to the database to obtain the information necessary to create a notification. The information is received in JSON format – from an API also developed within the project – and is further deconstructed and saved in a variable. The parameterization of notifications includes the regularity of the event (e.g., a sporadic appointment or a recurrent activity), which may be the exact day and time or the frequency (daily, weekly, monthly, or annually). According to the regularity of the event, certain moments to send notifications can be chosen, such as a week before, three days before, 30 min before, etc. The notification's message for each chosen moment can also be customized. In the case of a recurring event, after submitting the form to create an event and the respective parameters, one or several notifications are generated for a defined period.

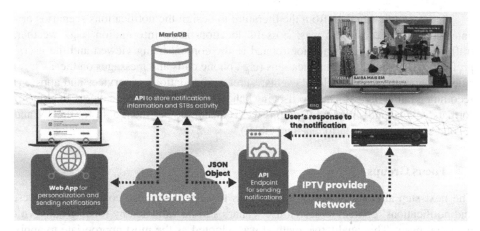

Fig. 1. OverTV system architecture.

All notifications are stored in a relational database – MariaDB (see Fig. 1). The insertion of information in the database is performed when a request is received from the user interface component (e.g., creation of a new user or new notification). By querying the database, it is possible to see if there are new notifications that should be sent and to which users. There are two types of triggers for sending notifications: i) time of sending, and ii) user actions (zapping, and turning the STB on/off).

Hence, the notifications are based on geo-referenced data and users' preferred content regarding information, entertainment, and services, as well as calendar and health reminders. The same event may generate several notifications depending on each thematic category's predefined settings (but customizable). These parameter settings are related to STB triggers and timings which were tested in the field trial.

3 Methodology

The research towards developing and evaluating a solution for personalized notifications for the TV ecosystem comprised three phases: 1) a literature review; 2) focus groups; and 3) a field trial. Each phase consolidated the definition of use scenarios for the use of notifications in the TV ecosystem – namely personalized content, presentation formats, user interactions, and delivery settings – to be validated in a field trial. The following subsections describe each phase and their main contributions to the proposed solution.

3.1 Literature Review

For the literature review about recent studies regarding the use of push notifications in the TV ecosystem [2], a query on the Scopus and the Web of Science databases was carried out, considering a timeframe from 2015 to the date of the query (April 2021). The sample of 25 articles was divided into two representative groups identified after the analysis: guidelines for notifications for the TV ecosystem; and notifications for senior audiences.

The more relevant data from the literature to design the notifications scenarios oriented to the TV ecosystem was: i) useful location-based information (e.g., weather, traffic, news, etc.); ii) information related to the content being viewed and the users' preferences; iii) social communications (e.g., phone calls and messages on the TV); iv) calendar appointments and local events; v) recommendations of services and apps; vi) recommendation of health and well-being behaviours and medication alerts. In terms of formats, textual and sound notifications were considered pertinent both for the TV and second screens (e.g., smartphone and tablet).

3.2 Focus Groups

The next step after the literature review was to systematize use contexts, audiences, and notifications' content to design use scenarios to be validated by focus groups with potential users. This qualitative method was adopted as the most appropriate to apply in an exploratory phase of the research, since it allows faster and more useful access to information in collective sessions, based on the discussion of different points of view [9]. The content analysis was based on the dimensions defined in the focus group script for each scenario and other topics highlighted in the participants' discourses.

After the design of scenarios and the planning of the sessions regarding data collection instruments and gathering of participants, two focus groups were carried out, one in January and the other in March 2022. Given the age specificities regarding daily routines and use of technological devices, the sample of 12 people (between 17 and 80 years old) was divided into two groups of six participants: Focus Group 1 (FG1) with young adults and adults [2], in which were presented a broader scope of scenarios and exploring different household dynamics; Focus Group 2 (FG2) with seniors (65+), in which were presented scenarios focused on social interaction through phone calls and messages on the TV, notifications about local events, and health monitoring.

The focus groups aimed to gather information about the relevance of those scenarios and to identify other use cases regarding the TV ecosystem at home. The scenarios were presented in video animations during a 60-min session in a setup with a living room configuration. Before the beginning of the session, each participant answered a brief characterization survey about audiovisual content consumption and the use of devices. After each scenario, participants manifested their opinions and mentioned suggestions for other notifications they would find useful.

Overall, the most-well received scenarios by the FG1 [2] were: 1) "Info", comprising notifications integrated into a morning routine with the information for the day and, an evening routine with information for the next day); 2) "Content", namely the discovery of unexplored TV channels and, social suggestions from friends regarding what they are currently watching and what they enjoyed watching; 3) "Services", allowing users to select apps they want to receive notifications from in the TV screen.

The opinions expressed by the FG2 showed a very high interest in TV notifications, confirming that the scenarios presented would contribute, respectively to: feeling less lonely by facilitating communication with family and friends through easy speech-to-text messages ("Social"); feeling more motivated to participate in local events by being able to invite and be invited by friends ("Calendar"); adopting healthier behaviours by reminding them of regular medication intake and health indexes monitoring, such as heart rate using smartwatches ("Health").

Although most of the suggestions for new scenarios were collected from the younger sample (FG1), TV notifications were better received and considered more facilitating of day-to-day life by the older participants (FG2). This audience, who spends more time at home and for whom the TV is the preferred device to keep them company, did not raise privacy issues or major concerns about interrupting the content being watched, except in the case of the broadcast of live football matches. On the contrary, for younger people, the lack of privacy and the interruption of programs with messages on TV, which they mentioned as causing anxiety, were the main problems identified for the notifications received on this shared device.

Based on the insights from the focus groups, the research proceeded to the development of a functional prototype of an iTV notification management platform. The solution was evaluated through a field trial and the results are reported in the following sections.

3.3 Field Trial

The main goals of the field trial were to understand how the users react to TV notifications at home and how useful the various thematic categories and delivery schedules were to their daily lives. After the user experience during the field trial, the goal was also to obtain suggestions for improvements and other typologies of notifications to be integrated into the next versions of the prototype.

The sample comprised 25 participants (see Fig. 2), 15 females (60%) and 10 males (40%), between ages 23 and 85 (average age 56). Despite the small size of the sample, the criteria to participate were being a subscriber of the STB service of the partner IPTV provider (MEO) and being available to participate in further stages of the study. Another important factor for the sample was including diversified household dynamics. Hence, the 25 participants (see Fig. 2) are distributed into 14 homes (each corresponding to an STB) with different compositions regarding age groups – young adults ($\leq$30), adults (31–64) and seniors (65+) – and households (singles, couples, families, and housemates).

Given the wide age range of the sample (23–85), some participants expressed in the pre-trial characterization survey difficulties using certain devices. Amongst the elder participants, 7 (28%) mentioned that they face difficulties using the smartphone, whilst 2 (8%) do not use this device at all. Regarding the tablet, 40% of the participants do not use it and 8% have difficulties doing so. Finally, 16% expressed difficulties using the computer and 28% do not use it at all. Regarding the TV consumption habits of the sample, 56% of the participants mentioned that they watch TV more than once a day, and 36% said they watch it once a day. Only one participant (4%) mentioned watching TV once a week and another participant watches once a month (4%).

The field trial was carried out for 44 days, between the months of July and August 2022. The evaluation protocol was divided into four stages: 1) the recruitment of participants and providing instructions about the proposed solution and the field trial; 2) filling out a pre-trial survey to characterize the sample regarding the usage of devices and TV consumption habits, and to gather users' preferences and information to create personalized notifications; 3) implementation of the field trial in the participants' homes, with permanent remote monitoring and technical support; 4) filling a post-trial

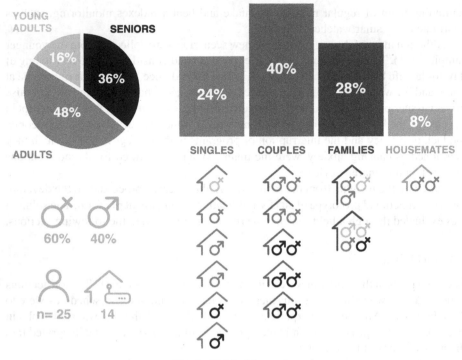

Fig. 2. Field trial sample.

survey to obtain feedback, namely about the receptivity to the service and the several thematic notifications, as well as the identifications of pain points and suggestions for improvements.

4 Field Trial Results

The results of the field trial were gathered through a post-trial survey and the statistics provided by the notification management platform, developed within the research project. From the requirements and scenarios most valued in the focus groups with potential users, the system tested in users' homes included five thematic categories of notifications: "Info", "Content", "Services", "Calendar", and "Health" (the "Social" category was not considered). Because the TV notifications followed the interface style and remote-control interactions of the IPTV partner, this study is not centred on design and usability metrics but on understanding if the notifications from several thematic categories and their different schedules were useful in the participants' daily lives. The results were divided into three subsections: i) the success of delivery rates and users' preferences; ii) the overall receptivity to the solution also according to age groups and households; iii) the limitations of the study followed by the participants' suggestions for improvements.

4.1 Notifications Delivery Rates and Users' Preferences

Within the proposed system of notifications, it is possible to distinguish two main types: *general notifications* and *personalized notifications* (see Fig. 3). The difference between the two is that *general notifications* are sent to everyone with the same content and schedule, while *personalized notifications* include the name of the user and information directed to that person (according to data and preferences previously provided by the participants through the pre-trial survey, using dedicated form fields for each type of customized information, corresponding to the thematic categories – e.g., regular medication; favourite TV shows; regular appointments and activities; preferred days to order food, etc.).

It is important to clarify that the system only considers that notifications were successfully sent if the user's TV STB was turned on. Nevertheless, it was not possible to confirm if and which user of the household viewed the notification. For this purpose, complementarily to the platforms' statistics, it was used the data from the post-trial survey considering the users' perceptions about the number of notifications they viewed and their usefulness per category (see Fig. 3).

Overall, throughout the field trial were created 4465 notifications, of which 72,5% were successfully sent (3693 notifications). When questioned about how many notifications they viewed, 32% of the users answered "more than 3 per day", while 8% said they "never saw any notification". Adding to these statistics, 64% of the participants considered that the number of notifications they saw every day was "adequate", and another 12% considered it "very adequate".

The *general notifications* include two regular *routines* with information about the date, weather forecast and daily news: the *morning routine* (6 am–12 am), in which 76,3% of the created notifications were successfully sent, and the *evening routine* (7 pm–12 pm), in which 84,5% of the notifications were also successfully sent. As shown in Fig. 3, the *routines* were the category with the highest percentage of received notifications (93,4%), particularly the *evening routine* (84,5%). This suggests that the evening period is more likely to have people watching TV or, at least, having the device turned on. In the post-trial survey, 48% of users expressed that the *routines* were "very useful" and 36% considered them "useful". However, 40% of the users considered particularly "useful" the daily *news* sent in the *mourning routine,* suggesting that this type of content may be more suited to the beginning of the day. This value might also have been influenced by 40% of users mentioning that they "did not receive any" *news* in the *evening routine.* This can be explained by several factors: the fact that the *routines* comprise a sequence of two or more "Info" notifications (and sometimes also "Calendar" notifications if it is the date of an event), and the users might not pay attention to all the queued notifications; the user may have the television connected but was not viewing TV or was not paying attention to the TV in the sending schedule; the system may have registered errors.

Figure 3 helps to understand which thematic categories were perceived as more useful, despite their successful delivery rates. For instance, the percentage of notifications sent in the category of "Services" was the highest (84,48%) among all the *personalized notifications,* although only 24% of the users considered it "useful" and 40% said that they "did not receive any" notification of this kind (only 5 households mentioned habits of ordering food, so it only was created notifications for those STBs). The success of

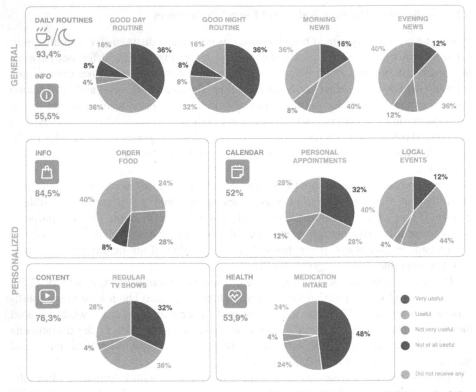

Fig. 3. Comparison by category of rates of sent notifications (platform statistics) and of the participants' perceived usefulness (pos-trial survey).

this delivery rate can be due to the schedule of the "Services" notifications being close to mealtime since they were only used in the field trial for ordering food services. This suggests the efficacy of these time slots for other categories.

The "Content" category had the second-best rate of notification delivery (76,3%). These notifications are displayed 5 min before the user's favourite shows start, allowing him to directly switch to the channel the program airs. Not every user mentioned having a TV show or content that they regularly watch on the TV, with most of them only mentioning channel preference. Still, considering that the "Content" notification is sent shortly before the users' most watched shows start, led to 32% of users found this category "very useful" and another 36% found it "useful", indicating a positive response to this strategy of regular habits timeslots.

The "Calendar" category had the lowest rate of sent notifications (52,03%). This might have happened because the sending parameters for the "Calendar" category were to send the notification when the user was zapping through channels and, complementary, also send it on the day and previous day of the event, integrated into the *morning routine* and the *evening routine*. Being the *routines'* schedule the most successful in terms of delivery rates is possible that the zapping trigger might have negatively impacted this value. However, despite the lower rate of delivery, 32% of users found the "Calendar" notifications to be "very useful". Also, 44% considered "useful" notifications that suggested *local events,* which is a type of notification also integrated into the "Calendar" category. Furthermore, 23,5% of the users mentioned they "attend to some of the suggested events" and 35,3% said they "did not attend but had an interest in attending", which shows that this type of notification can have a real impact on people's lives. Additionally, even users who said they "did not receive any" notification about *local events,* found this possibility interesting mentioning it in the post-trial survey open question asking for suggestions.

Finally, the "Health" category also showed a low percentage of successfully sent notifications. But, in terms of perceived usefulness, the *medication* notification (integrated into the "Health" category), presented the highest percentage of being considered "very useful" (48%), along with the *routines* (48%). The low rates of delivery of the "Health" category, namely the *medication* notifications corresponding to intake schedules, may be explained because the users were not watching TV during that period. This fact suggests the need for redundant notifications in personal mobile devices. Nevertheless, when asked on which devices they would prefer to receive notifications the majority preferred the shared television (56%), while 44% preferred exclusively mobile devices, and only 16% of the participants chose the option of integration of connected devices (e.g., TV, mobile devices, and smart assistants).

5   Receptivity to the Solution

As for the receptivity towards the proposed solution, the sample showed favourable scores, namely in terms of the following variables present in three questions of the post-trial survey: i) the adequacy of the presentation of the notification on the TV (86%); ii) the usefulness of the notifications received on TV (84%); and iii) the foreseen interest in using this notification service (80%).

Additionally, to better understand the influence that age groups and different household compositions have on these receptivity scores, non-parametric tests with a correction method for simulation were applied to check for trends applicable to other samples. Given that the studied sample is heterogeneous, the inferential analysis of these selected questions resorted to the application of non-parametric tests with the presentation of statistical data results reported in terms of p value, test power (rank) and frequency of respondents (N). To verify the independence between two variables, Pearson's chi-square test (X^2) was used, following the interpretation of rejecting the null hypothesis (H_0) if $Sig > \alpha = 0,05$ [10]. In cases where the application assumptions are infringed: a) there are no more than 20% of cells with an expected frequency of less than 5; b) there is no cell with a value less than 1, we resort to correction via the Monte Carlo simulation method. Also, the Adjusted Standardized Residuals are analyzed, in which classes with adjusted residuals lower than -2 (1,96) or higher than $+2$ (1,96) are sought, indicating significant differences in relation to H_0. In cases where the alternative hypothesis (H_1) is accepted, the measures of association based on the Chi-square test are verified: Phi and Cramér's V [10]. Additionally, to compare independent or unrelated groups, the Kruskal-Wallis (H) tests were used. The purpose of applying such tests is based on the ability to analyze the distribution of variables, allowing the verification of significant differences in the distribution, in which the null hypothesis of independence is rejected if the *p* value is less than $\propto = 0{,}05$ [10].

The Adequacy of the Presentation of the Notification on the TV. To the pos-trial survey question *"In terms of interference with what you are watching on TV, how do you consider the way notifications are presented?"* (see Fig. 4) the overall results showed that 56% of the sample considered it "very adequate" and 28% found it "adequate".

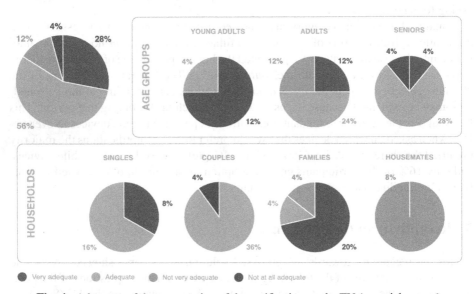

Fig. 4. Adequacy of the presentation of the notification on the TV (pos-trial survey).

Regarding the age group, the "young adults" were the ones with the response totally positive to the adequacy of the presentations of the notifications on the TV (12% "very adequate" and 4% "adequate"). By opposition, 4% of participants from the "seniors" group answered "not at all adequate" and 12% of participants from the "adults" group answered "not very adequate". As for household composition, the "singles" were the group with the response totally positive to this question (12% "very adequate" and 4% "adequate"), although the "families" group was the one with the highest scores regarding the answer "very adequate" (20%). Contrarywise, the 2 participants in the "housemates" group were unanimous considering the presentations of the notifications on the TV "not very adequate" (8%) and only one participant in the "couples" group (4%) considered them "not at all adequate".

The Usefulness of the Notifications Received on TV. To the pos-trial survey question *"In general, how do you consider the notifications you received on TV?"* (see Fig. 5) the overall results showed that 32% of the sample considered it "very useful" and 52% found it "useful".

Regarding the age group, one participant of each age group (4%), considered the notifications received on TV "not at all useful", and another participant of the "seniors" group found them "not very useful". More "adults" manifested a stronger conviction

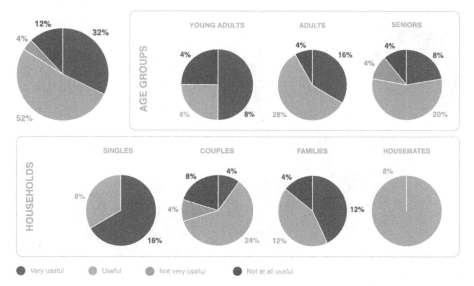

Fig. 5. Usefulness of the notifications received on TV (pos-trial survey).

considering the notifications on TV "very useful" (16%), although half of the "young adults" group (8%) also had the same opinion. As for household composition, the "singles" were the group with a response totally positive to the usefulness of notifications on TV (16% "very adequate" and 8% "adequate"), as well as the "housemates" (8% "adequate"). The "couples" was the group more doubtful about this usefulness (8% "not at all useful" and 4% "not very useful"), and also one participant of the "families" group (4% "not at all useful").

The Foreseen Interest in Using this Notifications Service. To the pos-trial survey question *"Considering your suggested improvements, how interested are you in using this service in the future?"* (see Fig. 6) the overall results showed that 20% of the sample is "very interested" and 60% are "interested".

Regarding the age group, the "young adults" were the ones with a totally positive interest in using the proposed notifications service in the future (8% "very interested" and 8% "interested"), although participants from the other two age groups were positively receptive, particularly 12% of the "adults" participants (12% "very interested"). By opposition, one participant of the "adults" (4%) and one of the seniors (4%), were "not at all interested" in using this service in the future, and another participant of the "seniors" was "not very interested". As for household composition, the "couples" were the group that showed more rejection of using the service in the future "not at all interested". But, in general, most households were receptive, namely the "housemates" group which was unanimous in being "interested" (8%), although the participants who claimed to be "very interested" were from the "families" (12%) and "singles" group (8%).

Finally, from the hypothesis of dependence between each of the three variables from the selected questions – the "adequacy" of presentation on the TV"; the "usefulness of the notifications on the TV", and the "interest in using the service in the future" – and the

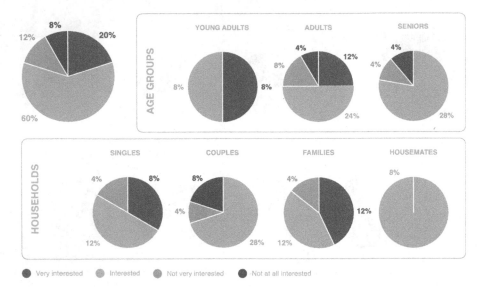

Fig. 6. Interest in using this notifications service in the future (pos-trial survey).

variables "age group" and the "household composition", only one case was confirmed. Both non-parametric tests confirmed the "perception of the adequacy of notifications presentation on the TV" proven significantly affected by "household composition". The age group dependency was not verified.

Through the Chi-square test resorting to correction via Monte Carlo simulation method, the dependence of the variable "households" on the "adequacy of notifications presentation" is verified ($X^2 = 29,974$; $p_{\text{Monte Carlo}} = 0,001$; N = 25). When confronted with the adjusted residuals, it demonstrates that there is an overvaluation by the "couples" and the "families" in relation to the scale degrees of agreement "very adequate" and "adequate". The Kruskal-Wallis test also proved the dependence of both variables (H(3) = 10,345, $p = 0,016$). Pairwise comparisons with adjusted p values showed that the difference between "housemates" ($M_{\text{rank}} = 23,00$) and "families" ($M_{\text{rank}} = 8,21$) was significant ($p = 0,031$).

This shows that the most positive perception of the adequacy of notifications presentation is more robust in the "families" household composition, both within the sample (Chi-square test resorting to correction via Monte Carlo) and as a tendency for other samples (Kruskal-Wallis test). Suggesting that collective viewing based on common routines and preferences involving the whole family is a relevant factor to consider when developing notification services for shared TV screens at home.

5.1 Limitations of the Study and Suggestions for Improvements

Along with the reduced sample size, due to inclusion criteria (being a subscriber of the IPTV partner's service and the availability to continue participating in subsequent field trials), one of the main limitations of the study is the impossibility of confirming if a user viewed the notification or whom of the household members is watching. Because there is no profile system on the TV and the notifications do not necessarily require user interaction and automatically disappear from the screen after 20 s. This is related to the reported technical problems during the field trial, namely: not receiving any notifications (43,5%); receiving many notifications in a row outside the correct time schedule (34,8%); and not being able to open the details of some notifications (17,4%).

The problem of accumulation of notifications (corrected still during the trial period) was due to a technical error registered when the users' TV was turned off, causing queuing of notifications followed by a bulk delivery when the TV was turned back on.

In the case of not receiving any or some notifications, the possible causes may be related to: the occasional use of the TV; not watching TV at the time of the notification delivery, which may suggest that the timeslot was not the most adequate; or not paying attention to the screen in the 20 s before the auto-dismiss of the notification. As for the users who claimed they did not receive any notifications, besides the aforementioned possible causes, it may be because many categories are personalized and dependent on information previously provided by the participants. So, if they did not provide, for example, medication schedules, calendar appointments or regular TV shows led to no notifications of these categories being generated for that user (although notifications of those categories may be displayed on the TV screen targeting other members of the household).

In view of the reported problems, the inclusion of a solution to identify who is watching the notification on the TV and the synchronization with mobile devices in the upcoming evaluation cycles will help to address most of the limitations found during the field trial. In addition, through open answers to the post-trial survey, the participants also had the opportunity to indicate improvements and suggestions for new types of notifications. These contributions were compiled into three groups: (i) presentation formats (possibility to activate sound alerts with the notifications; to have the size and positioning more similar to mobile devices notifications; (ii) sending schedules (to receive the notifications at fixed times, for example, when turning on the TV, or at a schedule defined by the user); (iii) other notifications (bill payments; movies that are showing in the cinema; alert of sports events of the user's sports club, for example, football matches; scheduling medical appointments; monitoring chronic diseases, for example, diabetes blood glucose control; mindfulness sessions and meditation exercises; display messages from family and friends on TV).

6 Final Considerations

The paper describes the research stages of developing and evaluating an iTV solution for sending personalized notifications. The study includes a literature review, the development of focus groups, and a field trial.

After the systematization of the literature review, use scenarios designed with an emphasis on home TV were presented in focus groups to discuss their relevance and collect further suggestions. The qualitative analysis of the focus group data provided significant insights for the prototyping stage, namely about the relevance given to the personalization of formats, preferred devices, and the intrusion moments for receiving the notifications. It also highlighted the differences between user profiles that seem related to age groups, viewing habits, use of connected devices, and household routines.

Subsequently, a field trial was carried out with a sample of 25 participants during a period of 44 days. This evaluation was focused on understanding if the categories and settings of the notifications were adequate and useful in the users' daily lives. Also, presents the comparison of the receptiveness to the solution according to different age groups and household compositions. The non-parametric Chi-square test resorting to correction via Monte Carlo and the Kruskal-Wallis test revealed the dependence between the variable of "adequacy of the presentation of the notifications" as not being disruptive of the content being viewed with the variable "households". The dependency between the variables was particularly significant in the "families" composition, which seems to suggest the relevance of considering collective viewing routines as a relevant factor when developing notification services for the TV.

Overall, there was a positive response to TV notifications in terms of the usefulness of the messages (85%) and a manifest willingness to use the service in the future (80%). Despite some low delivery rates registered during the field trial, which is associated with different schedules per category, the participants indicated the following preference of time slots to receive notification on the TV: after 7 pm (52%); when turning on the TV in the morning (36%); at lunchtime (24%); or after 10 pm (20%). Senior participants also indicated the afternoon period (20%) and the morning period (8%).

Even though the best rates of sent notifications are the *morning and evening routines* (93,4%) and *food delivery services* (84,48%), the highest percentages of perceived usefulness were assigned by users to *medication notification* (48%) integrated into the "Health" category, along with *notifications about local events* (44%) integrated into the "Calendar" category. Both the "Health" (53,9%) and "Calendar" (52,03%) categories were the ones with the lowest percentages of delivered, which may indicate problems with the timeslots since notifications are only successfully delivered if the TV STB is turned on. That does not necessarily mean that the user is paying attention to the TV screen or that other household member may have reacted to the notification since the television is still a shared device. But because both cases of *medication* intake and *appointments* have strict timings to be reminded, the way to avoid missing notifications when people are not watching TV or are not at home is the redundancy of sending the notifications also to mobile devices. Nevertheless, 56% of the participants indicated that they preferred receiving notifications on the home-shared television, whilst only 16% chose the option of receiving notifications on several devices at the same time. Because of the current prevalence and familiarity, 44% of the participants also indicated that they prefer to receive notifications exclusively on their mobile devices. Also, the field trial results suggested that user-activity-dependent sending parameters, such as zapping, may not be a good option. Because the only category that uses this mechanism is the "Calendar" which presented the lowest sending rate (52%).

In summary, the field trial validated all the categories included in the prototype, although with the need to fine-tune the sending schedules and delivery devices to increase the rate of successfully sent notifications. Participants also mentioned suggestions to integrate other notifications, such as bill payments, movies being shown in the cinema, and meditation sessions, among others. A subsequent field trial will be implemented for corroboration of the impact of optimizing sending times and testing the delivery of global and local trustworthy news rated with high credibility indexes through iTV notifications [11]. Other improvements demanding new iterations of the prototype, such as the inclusion of social features including phone calls and messages on the TV, the synchronization with mobile devices, and making the management platform available for users to autonomously create and schedule personalized notifications, will be addressed in upcoming evaluation stages.

Acknowledgements. Altice Labs@UA, a research group resulting from the partnership between Altice Portugal and the University of Aveiro, funded this research.

References

1. Business of Apps, Push Notifications Statistics. https://www.businessofapps.com/market place/push-notifications/research/push-notifications-statistics/. Accessed 18 May 2023
2. Velhinho, A., Camargo, J., Silva, T., Santos, R.: The importance of personalization and household dynamics for notifications in the TV ecosystem. In: Abásolo, M.J., Olmedo Cifuentes, G.F. (eds.) jAUTI 2021. CCIS, vol. 1597, pp. 3–19. Springer, Cham (2022). https://doi.org/10.1007/978-3-031-22210-8_1
3. Wheatley, D., Ferrer-Conill, R.: The temporal nature of mobile push notification alerts: a study of European news outlets' dissemination patterns. Digit. J. **9**, 694–714 (2021). https://doi.org/10.1080/21670811.2020.1799425
4. Silva, L.A., Leithardt, V.R., Rolim, C.O., González, G.V., Geyer, C.F.R., Silva, J.S.: PRISER: managing notification in multiples devices with data privacy support (2019). https://doi.org/10.3390/s19143098
5. Gavrila, C., Popescu, V., Fadda, M., Anedda, M., Murroni, M.: On the suitability of HbbTV for unified smart home experience. IEEE Trans. Broadcast. **67**, 253–262 (2021). https://doi.org/10.1109/TBC.2020.2977539
6. Amazon, Amazon Device Messaging (ADM) and local notifications on Fire TV. https://dev eloper.amazon.com/apps-and-games/blogs/2021/07/tutorial-amazon-device-messaging-on-fire-tv. Accessed 18 May 2023/
7. Netflix TechBlog, Rapid Event Notification System at Netflix. https://netflixtechblog.com/rapid-event-notification-system-at-netflix-6deb1d2b57d1. Accessed 18 May 2023
8. Encarnação, J., et al.: A management system to personalize notifications in the TV ecosystem. Procedia Comput. Sci. **219**, 674–679 (2023). https://doi.org/10.1016/j.procs.2023.01.338
9. Kruger, R.A., Casey, M.A.: Focus Groups. A Practical Guide for Applied Research. Sage, USA (2015)
10. Field, A.: Discovering Statistics Using IBM SPSS Statistics, 5th edn. Sage Publications (2018)
11. Encarnação, J., Velhinho, A., Bentes, S., Silva, T., Abreu, J., Santos, R.: Promoting trustworthy news through iTV notifications. In: Proceedings of the 14th International Multi-Conference on Complexity, Informatics and Cybernetics, IMCIC 2023, pp. 125–127. International Institute of Informatics and Cybernetics (2023). https://doi.org/10.54808/IMCIC2023.01.125

Combining Text-to-Speech Services with Conventional Voiceover for News Oralization

Marcelo Afonso⬥ and Pedro Almeida(✉)⬥

Digimedia, University of Aveiro, 3810-193 Aveiro, Portugal
{marcelo.afonso,almeida}@ua.pt

Abstract. The surge in digital content consumption has, in many cases, posed challenges for media companies, resulting in reduced revenue and the need to reinvent business models. The digitalization of content has introduced new consumption formats, and news podcasts have already become a reality in this landscape. While their existence is relatively recent in journalism, the increasing popularity of this format makes it an appealing addition to the field. But the production of podcasts may be demanding in what relates to the time, resources and even the technical expertise needed. In this scope, this paper primarily focuses on the premise of facilitating the creation of news podcasts. To achieve this, we propose employing Text-to-Speech technologies (TTS) for the oralization of journalistic texts in European Portuguese. We conducted tests using TTS services from Amazon Polly and Google Speech Cloud, with Google Speech Cloud Wavenet services yielding superior results among potential users. Additionally, we developed three podcast models incorporating human voiceover and/or TTS to get the users acceptance of those models. One model used only human voices, another only voice created with TTS and a hybrid podcast integrating both types of voices. The presence of human voice positively influenced the results, with the human voice model and hybrid voice outperforming the exclusive TTS voice model. However, the differences between the models were not significantly pronounced, and the results demonstrated an acceptance of Text-to-Speech technology in the context of news podcasts. Nonetheless, there remains a need for continuous technological advancement to converge with human discourse.

Keywords: Journalism · multimedia · automatism · digital · news · audio · voiceover · podcast · TTS · oralization

1 Introduction

This era marked the transition from traditional paper-based journalism to digital and online journalism. This implied and was result of changes in news consumption habits that lead to a significative reduction of revenue from physical copy sales and forced a reinvention of the prevailing business models in the journalism industry to ensure the funding of newsrooms [1]. The effort required for this adaptation affected newsrooms differently, depending on their ability to invest in modernization.

M. J. Abásolo et al. (Eds.): jAUTI 2022, CCIS 1820, pp. 68–79, 2023.
https://doi.org/10.1007/978-3-031-45611-4_5

The purpose of this paper is to explore the opportunities that arise from the emergence of new technologies that can reduce the costs associated with adapting journalism to new formats, particularly News Podcasts. The use of automated content production tools, specifically Text-to-Speech (TTS) conversion tools, is already a reality and has gradually been introduced in the field of journalism. In essence, TTS solutions enable the conversion of text into sound, simulating the human voice through phonetic algorithms that are increasingly comparable to natural speech due to advancements in technology. In the context of News Podcast production, these tools eliminate various stages and equipment that would otherwise be required, such as a speaker, sound capture equipment, and audio processing. This reduction in effort required to obtain news content can serve as a motivating factor for newsrooms seeking to convert their content without compromising quality. Therefore, it is crucial to understand how the public perceives these new tools and how News Podcasts incorporating this technology are received by consumers. The term "Podcast" was coined only 17 years ago, making it relatively recent in the chronology of journalism [2]. The understanding of this phenomenon and the development of a balanced model between conventional and synthesized expression are the guiding principles of this paper, with the aim of contributing to the evolution of digital journalism.

2 Theoretical Framework

Cyberjournalism has taken on a crucial role as a primary source for news consumption, becoming a regular part of our daily lives due to its user-friendly nature and adaptability across various devices [3]. The digitization of journalism, particularly in terms of consumption, appears to be a permanent trend. In Germany, for example, data from 2013–2020 reveals a 37% decline in the use of newspapers as the primary source of news, accompanied by a 21% growth in social media as a news source during the same period [4]. Portugal has also experienced a similar shift, resulting in reduced revenue for newspapers and a subsequent disinvestment in the Portuguese press, with a staggering 75% reduction in investment between 2006 and 2016 [5]. Media outlets have had to adapt their content production methods to cater to new digital consumption patterns [6].

One of the formats gaining significant traction in news content production is the audio format. In this adaptation process, Text-to-Speech (TTS) tools offer the ability to convert news articles into spoken words without the need for manual recording. With the emergence of news podcasts, TTS tools have become valuable aids in creating audiovisual content that complements news articles. The digital nature of podcasts allows for easy sharing on platforms that offer real-time and instant access to this type of content. Consequently, podcasts have experienced remarkable growth over the past decade [2]. Platforms like Spotify have witnessed a 24% increase in subscribers in 2020, largely due to the popularity of podcasts [7]. The category of news podcasts, in particular, has been expanding rapidly, with a 32% growth in the number of podcasts categorized as "news" between January and October 2019 alone [8]. In the United States, news podcasts were the second most listened-to genre in the second quarter of 2022, following closely behind comedy [9].

The use of TTS technology enables the elimination of several steps and equipment typically required for traditional news oralization or podcast production. This approach offers advantages for newsrooms that may lack the financial resources or time necessary for producing content in this format.

3 TTS Technology

TTS (Text-to-Speech) technology has undergone significant advancements since its introduction in the mid-19th century [10]. Presently, TTS systems aim to emulate the human voice by not only considering its auditory components but also capturing the idiosyncrasies and nuances of different types of voices [11]. These systems are progressively approaching the natural characteristics of human speech, employing complex processes like autoregressive modelling that require substantial computational resources [12]. The focus lies not only on creating intelligible synthetic speech but also on achieving a closer resemblance to human speech. This involves analysing sound wave characteristics and incorporating detected features into the final output generated by the system [13]. The evolution of TTS extends beyond mere synthetic vocalization and seems to converge with the human voice.

Speech synthesis systems can be categorized as parametric, concatenative, or neural. Parametric and concatenative systems dominated throughout most of the 20th century (Klatt 1987). The introduction of neural systems is a more recent development, specifically around 2010 [14].

As TTS technology evolves and approaches convergence with the human voice, its integration in news delivery processes becomes increasingly appealing to consumers. With improved naturalness, synthesized voices can be seamlessly incorporated into news podcasts, for instance. When choosing a TTS technology for a news podcast, the criterion of "naturalness" may seem obvious as one intends to select a TTS system that closely resembles the human voice. However, the subjective nature of the desired function plays a significant role in determining the best TTS technology [15]. Hence, it is necessary to adopt an appropriate methodology for evaluating and selecting the most suitable TTS solution.

3.1 TTS Technology Assessment

A TTS with the virtual assistant function may be evaluated differently from a TTS with the reading function [16]. Traditional TTS evaluation tests are based on the evaluation of sound samples. In these tests, participants evaluate unrelated and context-free samples and utterances. These tests have been contested for ignoring the real use of these TTS in the context in which they are applied or for the functionality they are proposed [15].

For the evaluation of synthetic speech systems, the method of MOS1 - Mean Opinion [17] was traditionally used. The MOS method was, for years, the standard for evaluating synthetic voices. However, with scientific advances, it seems to be limited as a single evaluation method [18]. In order to understand which aspects influence preferences, the authors Joseph Mendelson and Matthew Ayelett, propose a test that assesses the naturalness of the voice and its expressiveness [15]. For this purpose, the test uses voices with obvious differences in tone, with the aim being to evaluate the characteristics of naturalness and expressiveness from 1 to 5, depending on the MOS method. These sound samples are used in the same context with the reproduction of identical text excerpts. Thus, it is ensured that the participants interpret the best voice for the specific case presented to them and not the best voice in general [15].

Another case of innovation in the study of synthetic voices evaluates the TTS in different contexts, a priori declared, considering the function for which they are intended, but also the result of the interaction between the listener and the TTS in the case the function requires a response [16].

A comparative study [19] using 18 voices, including: Human Voices, Tacotron (Wavenet parallel project), Google Wavenet, Amazon Polly, Microsoft, Apple (iOS TTS), Android, among others, ranked the voices using the MOS method. Clarity, quality, and probability of hearing again were taken in consideration. This study determined that some TTS scored above one of the human voices, with the four highest scoring TTS being those using voices originating from Google Wavenet (Google Cloud Speech including Tacotron), followed by Microsoft TTS and Amazon Polly [19]. Some relevant aspects of this study are related to the principle that the same service, as is the case with Wavenet, can have a huge discrepancy between the qualification of the different voices available [19]. The same service can get impressive scores for one voice and frankly low scores for other voices. In view of this result, it seems to show that subjectivity is an inherent factor in the perception of the quality of the STT [16].

Considering the commercial offer in European Portuguese and the absence of comparative studies, the applicability of a TTS system for news reading or integration in a news podcast will always depend on the prior evaluation of which is the best TTS among those available for testing.

Subjectivity must necessarily be considered when assessing quality and, as such, there is the need to include more than one service at the time in tests. To date, Google Text-to-Speech services and Amazon Polly services are those that meet the best conditions for their applicability and best results in previously carried out comparative studies [19]. It should be noted that this specific study did not use European Portuguese versions for its assessments.

These TTS services are identical in the features provided: cloud operation, application via API, male and female voices, text entry via console with possibilities for modification via SSML and similar usage prices.

4   Methodology

The methodology employed in this study involves a theoretical approach to the focal question, followed by an experimental design phase that culminates in the development of prototypes aimed at addressing the problem addressed by this research. Three distinct phases were identified: firstly, the evaluation of a TTS service suitable for commercial application, enabling the conversion of news content from text to voice using European Portuguese Text-to-Speech (TTS) technology. Once the appropriate service was determined, the second phase involved creating news podcast models with varying degrees of TTS integration. Finally, the models were evaluated with a news podcast audience.

5 The Evaluation Process

5.1 First Evaluation

The intention, in this first phase, was to find out which TTS services were best received by the public. The services were evaluated using the conversion of a text excerpt, taken from a real news article to audio via TTS conversion. These excerpts were made available on an online survey platform. Six TTS solutions were evaluated (Table 1) - 2 services in European Portuguese of Portugal provided by Amazon Polly (Inês Polly (V3) and Cristiano Polly (V5)) and the 4 services provided by Google Cloud Speech WaveNet (pt-PT-Standard-A Wavenet (V1), pt-PT-Standard-C WaveNet (V2), pt-PT-Standard-B WaveNet (V4) and pt-PT-Standard-D WaveNet (V6)).

Table 1. Evaluated TTS Audio Services

Voice	Name	Duration	Voice Genre
1	pt-PT-Standard-A Wavenet	0:37	F
2	pt-PT-Standard-C WaveNet	0:37	M
3	Inês Polly	0:38	F
4	pt-PT-Standard-B WaveNet	0:37	M
5	Cristiano Polly	0:46	M
6	pt-PT-Standard-D WaveNet	0:37	F

The evaluation considered the following 5 characteristics: General Quality (Q1), Pronunciation (Q2), Pleasantness (Q3), Task compliance (Q4) and a final choice of the Favourite Voice for the News Oralization function (FV). The response options were placed in such a way that they could be converted to psychometric evaluation via the Likert scale [20]. The choice of the 6 TTS took into account the state of the art in previous comparative studies on TTS technology, namely the comparative study by [19] and the study on the perception of the quality of TTS [16]. The convenience sample included 53 respondents, 37 males and 16 females. The ages of the participants are between 19 and 65 years old, with an average of 30 years old ($M = 30$; $SD = 10.64$).

The voices with the best qualification in the parameters correspond to the voices that gathered the greatest preference (Voice 4–43.4% and Voice 6 26.4%) (Table 2). Although Voice 6 obtained a higher average in the individual parameters, in the final question about which voice is preferred, it was passed over by Voice 4. The two voices with the worst results belong to the Amazon Polly service (Voice 3 and Voice 5) The results show the differences between the two technologies in terms of their applicability for reading news in European Portuguese. Having identified the preferred voices, the study continued with the evaluation of podcast models that integrated TTS solutions.

Table 2. Summary table of results relating to the evaluation of TTS Services

	Q1	Q2	Q3	Q4	Average	FV
V1	3.26	3.77	3.04	3.06	3.28	5.70%
V2	3.79	4.32	3.55	3.55	3.8	15.10%
V3	2.47	3.19	2.36	2.49	2.63	7.50%
V4	3.89	4.47	3.75	3.89	**4**	**43.40%**
V5	2.23	2.85	2.32	2.21	2.4	1.90%
V6	3.94	4.53	3.83	3.90	**4.05**	**26.40%**

5.2 Creation of the Prototype Models

To conduct a comparative evaluation of the models, it was decided to create three distinct types of podcasts: one with a Real human voice (R), another with a Synthesized voice (S), and a Hybrid podcast that incorporated both human and synthesized voices (H).

The models were designed to enable a comparative analysis of the audience's perception of TTS technology, its added value, integration potential, and areas for improvement. Additionally, it aimed to gauge the acceptance of a hybrid model that could serve as a transition between conventional voiceover and an exclusive synthesized voice model.

After determining the models to be created, it was necessary to establish their structure and adapt them to a test environment with an audience. Therefore, it was envisioned that the created podcasts would faithfully replicate media content (news podcasts), where the conventional voiceover could be entirely replaced by a synthesized voiceover.

To better understand the structure of news podcasts, a survey was carried out based on news podcasts indexed in the "Top 200 Podcast Global News" on the "Chartable" website (available at: https://chartable.com/charts/chartable/podcasts-global-news-reach), whose measurement algorithm considers the total audience of each podcast, updated weekly. The first 10 podcasts that were part of this ranking between the 28th of April and the 4th of May 2021 were considered. Based on this survey, a common structure shared by most podcasts was identified and which was used for the creation of the prototypes. The models shared texts and a common base structure comprising an introductory jingle, background music, editorial material, sound separators, news content and an ending jingle.

The inclusion and selection of news underwent several stages. In the initial phase, regional news articles were chosen based on the guiding principles of the PressClub project, with a target duration of approximately 10 min. However, preliminary tests indicated that this duration would be excessive for user testing purposes. As a result, a new selection of journalistic content was made, focusing on the theme of innovation and new technologies. Three excerpts from news articles sourced from an online computer magazine were chosen.

Once the revisions were finalized, the texts were converted to audio using the Text-to-Speech conversion software from the Google Cloud Speech. Regarding the selection of synthesized voices, Voice 4 was chosen as it received the highest preference in the initial survey results. However, considering that the models included four speech segments (an introduction and three individual news segments), it was decided to also incorporate Voice 6, which exhibited the best results in the evaluated technical parameters. This choice ensured greater diversity for the prototype by combining both a male and a female voice.

Having the TTS synthesized voice model as reference, a real voice model was created using the same structure and texts to maintain consistency between the versions. The voiceover for this model was performed by a male content creator professional.

For the Hybrid version of the podcast, it was determined that the editorial material and a brief introduction to each news item would be read using human voiceover. As a result, the human voice accounts for 1 min of the total duration of the hybrid podcast's voiceover. The remaining 2 min and 35 s of voiceover are covered by the synthesized voice. Like the other models created, the remaining time is filled with pauses, entrance and exit jingles, and small sound separators.

5.3 Procedures for the Evaluation of Prototypes

Next, we proceeded with the analysis of the models combining text-to-speech with conventional voiceover. The primary focus was to gather information about the user experience in the context of news podcasts and to understand how the audience perceives and interprets the different text-to-speech conversion services and their integration with human voices.

The first part of the analysis involved evaluating the three models that combined text-to-speech services with conventional voiceover. This evaluation was conducted in a controlled environment using Plantronics BackBeat Pro 2 headphones, which provided external noise suppression. To ensure accuracy in identifying the nature of the voices, the sequence of listening to the podcasts was randomized, resulting in three possible orders: 1st order (1-2-3), 2nd order (2-3-1), and 3rd order (3-1-2).

Participants were not informed in advance about the nature of the voices they would hear, and visually, the podcasts were only identified in the survey as Podcast 1, Podcast 2, and Podcast 3. After listening to each podcast, participants were informed about which survey fields to complete. The interviewer controlled the sequence of podcasts that participants listened to during the session. The participants filled out the survey for the podcast they listened in the specified order before moving on to the next podcast.

In order to carry out an efficient evaluation of the generated models, it was decided to administer a survey with the following questions: *In relation to Podcast "x", what was the overall impression about what you heard*; *Regarding the voiceover of the Podcast "x", indicate the degree of suitability of the voices*; *Can the synthesized voice be used in the context of podcasts? State your degree of agreement*; The answer options for these three questions were placed to be expressed in a Likert scale. Finally, one last question was made: *Would you consider listening to a synthesized voice podcast in the future?*

Subsequently, an individual semi-structured interview was conducted, so that the participants could express their opinions about the models heard. The objective of this interview was to identify improvement opportunities related to TTS technology in the Context of News Podcasts.

5.4 Analysis of Results

Regarding the participants of this evaluation, it consisted of 15 individuals. About sampling, this was non-probabilistic for convenience. Regarding the gender of the participants, 8 (53%) identified themselves as men and 7 (47%) as women.

As for the **Overall Impression** and considering that the participants could select 5 possible answers: 5 Very satisfactory; 4 Satisfactory; 3 Normal; 2 Unsatisfactory; 1 Not satisfactory, we observed that the model with Real Voice gathered the highest values, with 4.27, followed by the Hybrid Voice Podcast with 4.07 and finally the model with Synthesized Voice with 3.93 as seen in Table 3.

Table 3. Overall Impression regarding the Podcast Models expressed in Likert Scale

	Hybrid	Real	Synthesized
Average	4.07	4.27	3.93
Median	4	4	4
Standard deviation	0.458	0.704	0.594

In relation to the **Voice Perception**, the Real Voice Podcast gathered the highest average value (4.07), followed by the Hybrid Voice (3.80) and finally the Synthesized Voice (3.67) as seen in Table 4.

Table 4. Voice Perception regarding the Podcast Models expressed in Likert Scale

	Hybrid	Real	Synthesized
Average	3.8	4.07	3.67
Median	4	4	4
Standard deviation	0.941	0.458	0.816

Out of the 45 obtained responses, only three tended to be negative. Two responses were marked as "Barely suitable" and one response was marked as "Not at all suitable". The "Barely suitable" response was selected for the Synthesized Voice Podcast, while the "Not at all suitable" option was chosen for the Hybrid Voice Podcast.

Regarding the **Identification of the Nature of the Voices** heard in the evaluated podcast models, we found that there was an average success rate of 66.66%. The success rate was 80% for the Hybrid Voice Podcast, 73.3% for the Real Voice Podcast, and 46.7% for the Synthesized Voice Podcast. It is import to highlight that three different sequences of podcasts were created and each third of the participants listened to one of the three sequences (1-2-3), (2-3-1), and (3-1-2). To further understand the influence of the listening sequence on participants' choices, cross tables were created (Table 5, Table 6 and Table 7), yielding the following results.

Table 5. Hybrid Podcast - Cross Table with Listened Order

	*	Real	Synthesized	**Synthesized and Real**	Total
Sequence	1 (1-2-3)	1	0	4	5
	2 (2-3-1)	0	1	4	5
	3 (3-1-2)	0	1	4	5
Total		1	2	12	15

Table 6. Real Voice Podcast - Cross Table with Listened Order

	*	**Real**	Synthesized	Synthesized and Real	Total
Sequence	1 (1-**2**-3)	5	0	0	5
	2 (**2**-3-1)	1	1	3	5
	3 (3-1-**2**)	5	0	0	5
Total		11	1	3	15

Table 7. Synthesized Voice Podcast - Cross Table with Listened Order

	*	Real	**Synthesized**	Synthesized and Real	Total
Sequence	1 (1-2-**3**)	0	4	1	5
	2 (2-**3**-1)	1	2	2	5
	3 (**3**-1-2)	0	1	4	5
Total		1	7	7	15

* 1- Hybrid Podcast | 2- Real Voice Podcast | 3 – Synthesized Podcast

Observing the results, we can see that regarding the Hybrid Podcast all sequences had the same 80% success rate, with two participants considering the voices heard as "Synthesized" voices and one participant considering the voices as "Real".

Those who started by precisely listening to podcast 2 "Real Voice" had only a 20% success rate, contrary to the remaining sequences with 100% success rates. Most people who listened to Podcast 2 in the first place considered that this podcast was composed of "Synthesized and Real" Voices, or in one case by "Synthesized" voices, and only one participant with this assigned sequence, got the right answer about the nature of the voices used.

Finally, in the last table (Table 7), we see that people who listened to Podcast 3 (Synthesized Voice) in last place had the highest hit rate (80%) and those who listened to Podcast 3 in first place had a rate of only 20% accuracy, with 4 of the participants considering that the voices heard were "synthesized and real". The remaining 5 participants who listened to this podcast in the second position, listening to the Real Voice Podcast in the first place, had a 40% accuracy rate, with 2 of the participants considering that the voices were "Synthesized and Real" and 1 participant to consider that the voices heard were "Real".

Regarding the possibility of using TTS voices in the context of news podcasts, respondents indicated an average agreement of 3.53 on a Likert scale. Approximately 66% of the answers given to this question (n = 10) were of positive agreement trend (Table 8).

Table 8. Agreement with the use of TTS in the Context of Podcasts (Likert Scale)

Average	3.53
Median	4.00
Standard deviation	1.125

The final question in the questionnaire pertained to the participants' willingness to listen to a synthesized voice podcast in the future. Upon analyzing the collected data, as presented in Table 9, it was found that 5 participants (33.3%) responded with "Yes," indicating their willingness to listen to a synthesized voice podcast in the future. On the other hand, 10 participants (66.7%) chose the option "Perhaps, after some improvements.".

Table 9. Would you consider listening to a synthesized voice podcast in the future?

	Freq	%
Yes	5	33.3
Perhaps, after some improvements	10	66.7
No	0	0
Total	**15**	**100**

It is important to mention in relation to this final question that none of the participants chose the "No" option, with all the answers being positive, which demonstrates an openness on the part of the sample of this study to the incorporation of TTS technology in a podcast context in the future.

6 Conclusion

Regarding European Portuguese voices, during the initial selection process that shaped the subsequent stages, it was found that voices 4 and 6 from the Google Cloud Speech service WaveNet received the highest preference (Voice 4–43.4% and Voice 6–26.4%).

These voices also received the highest scores in individual parameters. On the other hand, the voices from the Amazon Polly service obtained the lowest individual scores, showing some discrepancy compared to the WaveNet services.

In the Final Questionnaire, there was a clear tendency to accept the integration of Text-to-Speech (TTS) technology. The questionnaire revealed a preference for the convergence of TTS technology with real voices. Users emphasized the need for improvements in synthesized voices. It is clear there is a desire for TTS to closely resemble real voices, and the acceptance of synthesized voices seems to increase as they approach the quality of human voices. Validation tests of the models showed that models with a greater presence of human voice achieved higher scores. Both the real voice model and the hybrid voice model outperformed the TTS voice model in the analysed parameters, with the real voice model obtaining the highest scores (4.07). However, the differences between the values obtained by each model were minimal, with the hybrid voice model scoring 3.80 and the synthesized voice model scoring 3.67. Overall, all models demonstrated a very positive receptivity.

Based on these findings, it can be speculated that the success of synthesized voices in the context of news podcasts or news oralization depends on their degree of approximation to human voices rather than being purely synthetic voices with distinct characteristics. However, considering the limited differences in receptivity among the different voice types, there are identified opportunities for wider use of TTS solutions. This is further supported by the significant investments and improvements being made in these solutions. Following on the work of the research team in developing platforms that automatically generate content (audio and video) [21] and specifically a podcast creation platform [22] these findings will contribute for the integration of TTS features in this kind of platforms.

References

1. Harte, D., Howells, R., Williams, A.: Hyperlocal Journalism: The Decline of Local Newspapers and the Rise of Online Community News. Routledge, Milton Park (2018)
2. Newman, N., Gallo, N.: News podcasts and the opportunities for publishers (2019)
3. Allan, S.: Online News: Journalism and the Internet. McGraw-Hill Education, UK (2006)
4. Newman, N., Fletcher, R., Schulz, A., Andı, S., Nielsen, R.K.: Reuters institute digital news report 2020 (2020)
5. Botelho, M.: A crise dos jornais e do jornalismo. Meios & Publicidade (2017)
6. Stephens, M.: A History of News. Oxford University Press, Oxford (2007)
7. Sweney, M.: Spotify credits podcast popularity for 24% growth in subscribers | Spotify | The Guardian, 03 February 2021. https://www.theguardian.com/technology/2021/feb/03/spotify-podcast-popularity-24-percent-growth-subscribers. Accessed 23 Feb 2021
8. Bhattacharjee, M.: News podcasts grow by 32% as daily news shows become increasingly popular, reports Reuters | What's New in Publishing | Digital Publishing News, 10 December 2019. https://whatsnewinpublishing.com/news-podcasts-grow-by-32-as-daily-news-shows-become-increasingly-popular-reports-reuters/. Accessed 23 Feb 2021
9. Edison Media: Comedy Tops the Podcast Genre Chart in the U.S. for Q2 2022 - Edison Research. https://www.edisonresearch.com/comedy-tops-the-podcast-genre-chart-in-the-u-s-for-q2-2022/. Accessed 05 Nov 2022

10. Klatt, D.H.: Review of text-to-speech conversion for English. J. Acoust. Soc. Am. **82**(3), 737–793 (1987)
11. Arik, S.O., et al.: Deep voice: real-time neural text-to-speech. arXiv preprint arXiv:1702. 07825 (2017)
12. Tian, Q., Wan, X., Liu, S.: Generative adversarial network based speaker adaptation for high fidelity waveNet vocoder (2019). https://arxiv.org/pdf/1812.02339.pdf. Accessed 09 Feb 2021
13. Gibiansky, A., et al.: Deep voice 2: multi-speaker neural text-to-speech. Adv. Neural. Inf. Process. Syst. **30**, 2962–2970 (2017)
14. Rowan, D.: DeepMind: inside Google's groundbreaking artificial intelligence startup | WIRED UK, 22 June 2015. https://www.wired.co.uk/article/deepmind. Accessed 08 Feb 2021
15. Mendelson, J., Aylett, M.P. Beyond the listening test: an interactive approach to TTS evaluation. In: INTERSPEECH, pp. 249–253 (2017)
16. Wagner, P., et al.: Speech synthesis evaluation—state-of-the-art assessment and suggestion for a novel research program. In: Proceedings of the 10th Speech Synthesis Workshop (SSW10) (2019)
17. Rec, I.: P. 85. A method for subjective performance assessment of the quality of speech voice output devices. Int. Telecommun. Union Geneva (1994)
18. Hoβfeld, T., Schatz, R., Egger, S.: SOS: the MOS is not enough! In: 2011 Third International Workshop on Quality of Multimedia Experience, pp. 131–136. IEEE (2011)
19. Cambre, J., Maddock, J., Tsai, J., Colnago, J.: Choice of voices: a large-scale evaluation of text-to-speech voice quality for long-form content, vol. 20, April 2020. https://doi.org/10. 1145/3313831.3376789
20. Likert, R.: A technique for the measurement of attitudes. Arch. Psychol. (1932)
21. Almeida, P., Beça, P., Soares, J., Soares, B.: MixMyVisit – a solution for the automatic creation of videos to enhance the visitors' experience. In: Abásolo, M.J., Olmedo Cifuentes, G.F. (eds.) jAUTI 2021. CCIS, vol. 1597, pp. 105–118. Springer, Cham (2022). https://doi.org/10.1007/ 978-3-031-22210-8_7
22. Almeida, P., Beça, P., Silva, T., Afonso, M., Covalenco, I., Duarte Nicolau, C.: A podcast creation platform to support news corporations: results from UX evaluation. In: ACM International Conference on Interactive Media Experiences, pp. 343–348, June 2022

e-Inclusion

iTV to Connect Generations: A Field Trial of a Solution to Send Personalized Notifications

Juliana Camargo(✉) ⓘ, Telmo Silva ⓘ, and Jorge Ferraz de Abreu ⓘ

DigiMedia, Department of Communication and Arts, University of Aveiro, Aveiro, Portugal
{julianacamargo,tsilva,jfa}@ua.pt

Abstract. Digital exclusion is part of the list of reasons that amplify older adults' social isolation and loneliness. Since they are not digital natives, like the newer generations, frequently these individuals do not have the same easiness to exchange messages or use other tools to connect them with other people. In this sense, the present work aims to identify whether the use of television to show personalized notifications, as an intermediary device, can boost interactions between the elderly and other generations since it is a familiar gadget to this audience. For this, a focus group was made with six participants, between 64 and 81 years old, who evaluated different scenarios centered on sending notifications to the television screen, suggesting actions that culminated in social interaction. Then, a platform that sends notifications to the TV was developed and subsequently used by 12 older adults (between 58 and 85 years old) for 44 consecutive days. This paper presents the results obtained during the tests conducted in the participants' homes and demonstrates that notifications displayed on the TV (a very familiar device for this audience) can enhance intergenerational connections, reducing the perception of social isolation and loneliness among older adults.

Keywords: older adults · push notifications · social isolation · TV · iTV, connect generations

1 Introduction

Population ageing is one of the main current concerns of organizations such as the World Health Organization (WHO) and the United Nations (UN) [1, 2]. There are currently 1.1 billion people over 60 years of age in the world, equivalent to 13.9% of the population [1]. All countries in general have seen exponential growth in the proportion of citizens in recent years and the projection by 2030 expected are, 1 in 6 inhabitants are 60 years or older [1]. This scenario highlights the importance of investing in policies, projects and initiatives capable of inserting this public into society, ensuring autonomy and inclusion. In this sense, according to the WHO [1], technological resources, such as the internet and mobile devices, are essential for this to happen. Although they are individuals more likely to have resistance to innovation [3], democratizing and fostering access is crucial to ensure a healthier and more active life [1].

Television, in turn, plays an important role in this context because it is a device widely used by the elderly [4]. It is also the main leisure activity of this group of individuals due

© The Author(s), under exclusive license to Springer Nature Switzerland AG 2023
M. J. Abásolo et al. (Eds.): jAUTI 2022, CCIS 1820, pp. 83–97, 2023.
https://doi.org/10.1007/978-3-031-45611-4_6

to accessibility and the fact that it does not involve barriers to its use [5]. The gadget is also considered a kind of company, especially for those suffering from loneliness and/or social isolation – only in Portugal, for example, 44,400 older adults are living in these conditions [6]. During the most critical phase of the pandemic caused by Covid-19, 16% of Portuguese individuals over 65 years old stated they spent more time in front of the TV precisely to alleviate this type of feeling [7].

This paper, therefore, connects these three aspects: seniors, TV and reduction of social isolation/loneliness rates. The objective is to identify whether integrating television features that facilitate access to technological resources can make their use simpler and, consequently, reduce the rates of social isolation. For this, we sought to understand the perception of the senior individuals themselves about the theme and the potential of television to expand contact with friends and family. Historically, television has been considered a companion for senior citizens. But is it possible to go beyond that, using it as a means of communication capable of facilitating access to technology and communication with their relatives? This work precisely seeks an answer to this question. Therefore, there has been a careful effort to listen and present possibilities for the target audience.

To present the findings, this paper was divided into four sections: following this introduction, there is the related work, which presents studies focused on the use of notifications and technological resources aimed at promoting social interactions and healthcare. In sequence, the two phases of the empirical work are detailed: the focus group and the field test, with their results being discussed throughout the section. Finally, there are the conclusions drawn based on the analysis of the results, followed by a description of future work.

2 Related work

Previous studies [8–12] showed that notifications can be mechanisms with great potential to stimulate the use of technological resources and interaction with family members, caregivers and friends. Overall, these studies have presented evidence that notifications (or reminders) have the potential to facilitate access to technology and promote interaction between older adults and individuals from other generations.

In [8] specifically, three older adults were encouraged to test a prototype that consisted of an adapted version of Facebook for television. According to the obtained results, the use of the application on TV, a device widely recognized by this demographic, facilitated the acceptance of the solution. Additionally, it provided a simpler and more intuitive experience for participants, fostering communication with their family and friends. A similar outcome was observed in study [9], where a virtual calendar specifically designed for seniors was created. For the 21 study participants, engaging with this type of technology increased their personal awareness of existing commitments, such as social events, birthdays, and important dates in general. This serves as an indicator of the potential for technology to integrate older adults into society and, consequently, bridge the generational gap.

Notifications also proved to be a crucial mechanism for promoting socialization among the elderly with hearing impairments. In [20], senior participants utilized a system that sent a message to their television to notify them of incoming calls on their mobile phones. Upon receiving the notification, the elderly individuals would answer the call and then use a prototype that transcribed the entire conversation. As the dialogues unfolded, the phrases were displayed directly on the television screen for easy reading. Overall, user feedback was positive, confirming that television is a device capable of facilitating access and viewing of this type of message. The three main reasons for this are: i) it is a technology with which they are familiar [8]; ii) they typically spend more time in front of this type of screen [19]; and iii) the larger screen size is also beneficial in this context [20].

The studies mentioned above are also part of a systematic review conducted specifically in this field [19]. Twenty-nine relevant papers were identified and thoroughly analyzed to assess the potential of notifications in connecting people. Overall, the findings indicated that messages facilitated communication between senior individuals and their families, particularly in the realms of "social," "health," and "teaching-learning". Specifically, three studies [8–10] reported that participants felt more "accompanied" during the testing period of the prototypes they were exposed to. All three projects concluded that notifications "have a high potential to connect people".

Additionally, in [21], a TV application was developed to enable older adults to request assistance from volunteers when needed, whether it's for shopping at the supermarket or performing specific household tasks. Voice resources were utilized as the primary input method to facilitate requests and interactions. The process unfolds in stages: i) the elderly access the application and initiate an automatic connection to their mobile phone; ii) they listen to the automatic message and are prompted to state their request after a beep; iii) they then hang up the call; iv) within the application, they can view the request and confirm their intention to send it to the network of volunteers. Feedback on the service provided by volunteers can also be provided via voice, following the same logic. The volunteer team receives this feedback first, makes any necessary corrections, and then makes it available to the user through the iTV application. This resource serves as an example of how television can mediate social interactions, thus reducing levels of loneliness and/or social isolation.

These studies mentioned here show that television can be an intermediary device for messages and notifications. It is considered that these are important indications that using it also in a social sense, to send messages that suggest interactions with family and friends, can be an interesting path to bring generations closer together.

3 Empirical Research

The study presented in this paper was conducted in several stages. Firstly, the studies identified in the systematic review [19] supported the development of a questionnaire, which was administered to 20 older adults (9 Portuguese and 11 Brazilian) – the results of which were also presented in [19]. The conclusions drawn from the participants' responses indicate that using TV as an intermediary for interactions through notifications is an effective way to promote social connections, particularly among older adults who widely use this device.

Based on the questionnaire responses, three scenarios related to intergenerational connections were identified and subsequently presented in a focus group involving 6 older adults recommended by the Senior University of Cacia in Portugal.

Finally, the insights gathered from the focus group guided the development of an actual platform enabling notifications to be sent to the television. This solution was subsequently tested with a group of 12 older adults, and the results of this testing are presented throughout this paper.

3.1 Procedure and Sample Characterization

The focus group on the use of television notifications was held in March 2022 at the University of Aveiro. It took place in a User Experience (UX) laboratory designed to simulate a real living room. The session lasted a total of 1 h and 36 min. Six individuals between the ages of 64 and 80 participated, along with two moderators and a professor from the Senior University of Cacia. The session began with an introduction to the topic and the request for participants to sign an informed consent form.

The moderators then asked each participant to briefly introduce themselves, including their names, ages, television consumption habits, and their overall relationship with technology. Rather than using written questionnaires, an oral presentation format was chosen to avoid tiring the participants with online or written tasks.

Next, three scenarios related to the use of television notifications were presented. Two scenarios focused on the interaction of seniors with other people, such as family members, caregivers, and friends, while one scenario focused on health promotion. The scenarios were represented through animated videos, each lasting approximately 15 s. The videos simulated the use of the notification mechanism on television, with a visual style designed to closely resemble reality, making it easier for the participants to understand. After each video, a set of 4 to 6 open-ended questions were asked to gauge the participants' level of acceptance of the proposals. Examples of questions included: "Do you find this scenario useful?" "Would you use this kind of functionality?" and "Do you believe this resource would help you connect with your family members?".

Towards the end of the session, a graphical representation of all the scenarios was displayed on the television screen to serve as a reminder and stimulate a discussion about other proposals and potential improvements to the options presented.

In terms of television consumption habits, all participants mentioned that they watch television every day. Only two individuals mentioned that they watch it less frequently, with one of them having difficulty with their vision. When asked about the types of content they watch the most, all participants mentioned "TV news". Additionally, two participants mentioned "documentaries" (2 times), "movies" (2 times), "entertainment programs" (1 time), and "sports" (1 time). Two participants mentioned that they engage in other activities while watching television, such as "playing crossword puzzles" or "doing crafts," but keep the device on for background noise. One participant also mentioned keeping the TV on in different rooms as a way to feel accompanied throughout the day.

Regarding the use of other technologies, all participants mentioned owning a mobile phone. However, only two individuals reported using their phones solely for making or receiving calls. The remaining four participants use their phones daily for messaging, accessing social networks, and making video calls. In addition to phones, three participants mentioned owning a computer, one mentioned having a tablet, and another mentioned having a smartwatch.

3.2   Focus Group: Seniors' Perception of the Use of Television Notifications

As mentioned, three scenarios were presented to analyze the levels of acceptance and preferences among the group of older adults' individuals regarding the use of notifications on television. All scenarios, as shown in Fig. 1, promote social interaction between the elderly and other generations. The objective was to examine whether the messages displayed on television contribute to integrating people of different ages in any way.

Fig. 1. Scenarios presented to participants.

Scenario 1: TV Call Notification

Focused on the social aspect, Scenario 1 presented a notification on the TV informing the elderly user that she was receiving a call from her granddaughter on the phone. The message suggested that she say "ok" out loud to answer the call, as the phone was configured to automatically answer calls when the activation word was recognized.

In general consensus, the participants found this functionality to be useful. Here are some examples of statements made by the participants: "It's a way to know that the phone is ringing even when we're not near it, which happens quite often to me" (Participant 4 -

P4); "It's very practical, especially for those with a large house or when the phone is not always within reach" (P5); "It's a feature I often use on my smartwatch and I really like it. It would be interesting to receive this type of notification on the television as well" (P4); "I often miss my son's calls because I'm busy with other things and we end up not talking. I think this functionality would help avoid this problem" (P1).

Initially, there was some difficulty in understanding whether the calls would be answered through the television or directly on the phone. It was necessary to intervene and explain the scenario again, emphasizing that the notification only served as a reminder about the call received on the phone. However, some participants took this opportunity to express their desire to receive and make video calls through the television. "That way, my husband and I could talk to our children at the same time. Doubtless, we would communicate more frequently during the week if we had this kind of feature," commented P2. Another aspect that was highlighted, this time by P1, was the potential convenience of answering calls using the television. "We are already familiar with the device, much more than with the mobile phone. I think it would be easier to use and we would communicate more frequently with those who are far away," they said.

Regarding content interruptions, the majority of the group stated that receiving such a notification would not be intrusive or uncomfortable, even if it occurred during a TV program, football match, or movie. Only one participant (P5) mentioned that they would not want to answer a call if the notification came during a football match, especially if it interrupted the content.

Scenario 2: Exchanging Messages with Family Members

In scenario 2, which also focuses on the social aspect, an example of intergenerational communication between a grandmother and her granddaughter is presented. The young woman uses her phone to send a message to the elderly lady expressing that she misses her. The content is displayed on the TV screen through a notification. By pressing the "ok" button on the remote control, the user can easily respond to the message by sending a heart emoji directly to the initiator's phone.

The group unanimously found the functionality "very interesting," particularly because it can facilitate interaction with family and friends. Here are some examples of comments made by the participants: "It's something I would use because it's very simple to interact with" (P5); "Not having to type to respond makes interaction easier" (P1); "It's a way to be closer to family in a very simple way" (P3); "With my children living abroad, receiving these notifications is a way to see that they remember me during the day. Undoubtedly, it helps alleviate the longing" (P4). The same participant mentioned that it would be beneficial for the notifications to be preceded by audible alerts. "That way, it would grab our attention if we were engaged in other activities," she said.

In general, the group approved this type of functionality due to its practicality (simply pressing "ok" to send a heart emoji), indicating that television can enhance intergenerational communication. They also expressed that they felt "less alone" when receiving and interacting with messages in a simple and practical manner.

Scenario 3: Health Monitoring
In this scenario, the focus is on health monitoring, which is one of the most critical characteristics for individuals living alone or experiencing social isolation. Various studies conducted in this context [15–18] demonstrate that TV notifications contribute to bridging the gap between family members and caregivers, ensuring closer monitoring.

The presented scenario consists of an integrated system with a smartwatch that detects high heart rate and automatically sends a notification to the television, asking if the user has taken their regular medication. The same messages are sent to the smartphones of family members and caregivers, ensuring closer monitoring.

From the outset, P1 and P3 emphasized the importance of this feature, especially for those who struggle with forgetfulness. "For those who use pill organizers with separate compartments for each day of the week, receiving a reminder like this would prompt them to check if they have taken their medication correctly," stated P2.

Most participants reported taking medication daily and acknowledged that a reminder system could help prevent forgetfulness, especially if the reminders appeared on television. They also mentioned how easy it is to forget to take the medication. P4 even utilizes technology to remind herself. "I set alarms on my phone and smartwatch to remind me about taking important medication," she said.

While recognizing the usefulness of this functionality, P5 pointed out that merely questioning the user about medication intake could have adverse effects. For example, it may cause confusion and lead the elderly to mistakenly ingest the medication again or be unclear about which medication should be taken at the exact time of the notification. "If I've already taken my medication and then I'm questioned, it can mislead me. I believe this feature needs some fine-tuning," commented P5. P6 agreed that some adjustments might be necessary but expressed interest in the functionality, considering it "very important". The group, in consensus, highlighted the importance of having clear and unambiguous message content to avoid confusion.

Finally, when asked if they would use the smartwatch to monitor their heart rate, all participants expressed that they would have no issue using it on a daily basis.

3.3 Field Trial

The methodology used to develop a platform dedicated to send notifications involved conducting a literature review and collecting empirical data through two focus groups (one with older adults, described in the previous section, and one with individuals from other generations). These activities allowed for the organization of scenarios and the definition of notification parameters. The implementation phase of the digital solution, as described in [22], was guided by these aspects.

Both focus groups, including the one with participants mentioned in the previous section, provided validation and identification of important aspects, such as specific content scenarios, optimal moments for receiving messages, preferred formats, and customization options.

Based on the requirements valued by the focus group participants, the systematization of the six notification categories was established. These categories are as follows:

1. **Info:** important information relevant to the daily lives of the elderly, such as weather and traffic conditions.
2. **Calendar:** reminders for upcoming events, including cultural programs, doctor's appointments, and birthdays of loved ones.
3. **Content:** information and reminders related to programs commonly watched by the users.
4. **Services:** suggestions for delivery services.
5. **Health:** reminders related to medication intake and other health-promoting activities, such as reminders to drink water and take exercise breaks.
6. **Social:** messages that encourage interaction between the elderly and their families, friends, and caregivers.

Developed in collaboration between the research team and MEO, a Portuguese IPTV provider, the solution aims to test the effectiveness of these types of messages with the older adults. The platform consists of two main components: a website for managing notifications, where personalized and programmed messages are created by the manager team based on each user's profile, and an interface that displays notifications on the television using the infrastructure provided by the partner provider (Figure 2 depicts the moment when a participant receives a notification).

Fig. 2. Notification displayed on the television.

To better understand the proposed solution, Fig. 3 provides context for the system's user interfaces (UIs) associated with the tasks that managers and users can perform. On the left, there is an image of the web platform, while on the right (above), there are two more examples illustrating how the public is impacted by notifications. Below, there is a definition of all the categories that have been created.

To evaluate the perception of the elderly towards the solution, a prototype was tested over a period of 44 days (from July 17 to August 31, 2022) in the homes of 12 individuals aged between 58 and 85 years old (the study was developed in compliance with the General Data Protection Regulation – GDPR). The average age of the participants is

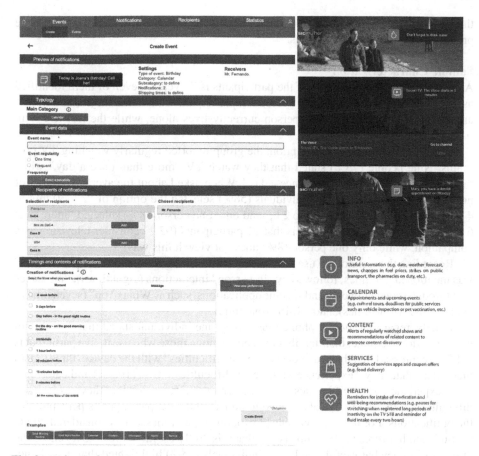

Fig. 3. Web platform for scheduling notifications (left) and interface for notifications and descriptions of message categories (right).

74 years. It is important to note that this sample was chosen for convenience and is different from the one that took part in the focus group described in the previous section.

During this testing period, various notifications were programmed to suggest actions aimed at promoting socialization, categorized as "Social" and "Agenda". Here are some examples of the messages sent to the participants:

1. "Do you miss your granddaughter Anna? How about giving her a call?"
2. "Today is your daughter Mary's birthday! How about sending her a message?"
3. "Do you miss Mary? How about scheduling something with her over the weekend?"
4. "On July 18th, there is a party in the parish of Mafamude, in Vila Nova de Gaia. Would you like to know more about the event?"

After using the platform and receiving these messages frequently, the participants were asked to complete a questionnaire. The questionnaire aimed to understand if the solution effectively motivated them to take the proposed actions and whether it made them feel closer to their family and friends. The detailed results of the questionnaire are presented in the following sections.

Sample Characterization

As mentioned, the average age of the participants is 74 years. Seven of them identified as female (58%) and five as male (42%). All participants stated that they have children and/or grandchildren. Only one person currently lives alone, while the rest live with partners or relatives.

In terms of television consumption, the group reported regularly watching TV programs. Nine people (75%) stated that they watch TV "more than once a day," while three (25%) said they watch it "once a day". When asked about the average number of hours watched per day, seven individuals (58%) selected the option of "2 h 30 min to 4 h," four (33%) chose "30 min to 2 h," and only one person (8%) selected "more than 6 h". Another significant finding is that 11 participants (92%) consider television as a companion, while only one person (8%) does not view it this way.

Regarding the technology used to connect with their family members, "phone calls" was mentioned ten times, followed by "in-person" interactions (eight times), "messages sent through social networks and specific applications, such as WhatsApp" (seven times), "video calls" (four times), and "SMS" (one time).

Finally, regarding mobile phone usage, only one individual stated that they do not use the device to contact their family members. Among those who use it, five participants (41.7%) expressed that they "do not experience difficulties" with the device, three (25%) mentioned that they "experience significant difficulties," two (16.7%) indicated that they "experience some difficulties," and one person (8.3%) stated that they "experience difficulties all the time". We also aimed to understand each participant's perception of the notifications. For three individuals (25%), this type of message is considered "quite useful"; another three (25%) emphasized that it is "fully useful"; three (25%) chose the option of "somewhat useful," and three individuals (25%) highlighted that they do not usually receive such notifications.

Discussion of Results

The results of the field test combined the statistics provided by the notification management platform with the data obtained from in-person interviews conducted with the participants. After the testing period, a questionnaire focused on the perceived usefulness of the proposed solution, particularly in promoting social interactions, was administered. It is important to note that the usability of the system was not evaluated in this study, as the design of the notifications followed a standard set by the TV operator.

During the testing period (a total of 44 days), 902 notifications were sent in the categories of "agenda" and "social". The "agenda" category included reminders for birthdays, appointments, and local events, while the "social" category aimed to encourage intergenerational interactions through telephone calls and text messages.

Out of the total volume of notifications, 435 (48.22%) were not delivered to users because their television sets were not turned on at the time of delivery. This played a significant role in the receipt of the scheduled messages. Overall, the acceptance of messages received in the "social" and "agenda" categories was positive (Table 1).

Table 1. Percentage of notifications received, usability perceptions, and actions taken by study participants

Rates of received notifications	Highlights of rates of perceived usefulness	Actions taken[a]
Encouraging calls and messaging		
67.5%	16.7% "very useful" 33.3% "useful" 50% "did not receive any"	66.7% "I called after receiving the notification" 33.3% "I didn't call, but I felt like calling"
Birthdays and special dates (calendar)		
77.3%	16.7% "very useful" 25% "useful" 8.3% "useless" 50% "did not receive any"	50% - "I called my family after receiving the notification." 33.3% - "I didn't call, but I felt the urge to do so." 16.7% - "I didn't call, and I didn't feel the urge to do so."
Local Events		
62.3%	50% "useful" 50% "did not receive any"	33.3% - "I didn't participate, but I felt the desire to do so." 16.7% - "I participated." 50% - "I had no interest in participating."

[a]The percentages of the third column are only based on the 50% of participants that received the messages.

The analysis of Table 1 reveals that a majority of the individuals who were impacted by the notifications suggesting sending messages and making telephone calls actually carried out these actions. Those who did not still expressed a desire to do so. In terms of acceptance, 16.7% (4) classified the notifications as "very useful," and 33.3% (2) as "useful" (50%, or 6 individuals, reported not receiving them). These indicate that the older adults are not indifferent to this type of mechanism, highlighting its potential to impact and stimulate intergenerational connections.

Regarding the birthday alerts sent during the testing period, 3 participants (25%) found the messages "useful," 2 (16.7%) considered them "very useful," 1 (8.3%) deemed them "useless," and 6 (50%) stated that they did not receive them. Among those who did receive them, 3 out of 6 (50%) actually made a call to wish the birthday person a happy birthday. Another 2 out of 6 (33.3%) expressed a desire to call or send a message to their loved ones upon receiving the notification. For 1 out of 6 (16.7%) who received the notification, it was not a motivating factor. However, all individuals impacted by this type of message expressed feeling "closer to their families" (as reported by five individuals) or "much closer to their family" (as reported by one individual).

About notifications about local events, 6 individuals (50%) found them "useful," while another 6 (50%) reported not receiving such messages. Among the participants who received these reminders (6), 1 individual (16.7%) stated that they actively participated in the indicated event, and 2 (33.3%) indicated that they did not participate but felt inclined to attend. Additionally, 5 participants (83.3%) highlighted that these messages made them feel more "connected to the community where they live," and 1 (16.7%) emphasized feeling "much closer to their community".

These facts indicate that most of the older adults impacted by the notifications were not indifferent to them. Many of them took the suggested actions, reinforcing two important points: a) the television can be a device that facilitates access to this type of content/interaction, and b) notifications sent to TV have the potential to promote intergenerational connections.

In this regard, it was also important to evaluate whether the proposed system brought significant changes to the daily lives of the elderly, particularly in terms of their perception of social isolation and loneliness. The evaluation was based on their responses to the following question, which utilized a loneliness scale ranging from 1 to 7:

"How do you feel?"
Fully accompanied; ii) Quite accompanied; iii) Somewhat accompanied, iv) Neither alone nor accompanied; v) Somewhat alone; vi) Quite alone, and vii) Totally alone.

This question was posed to all study participants at two key moments: before the tests and after 44 days of system usage. Changes in their responses were examined and are easily identified in Table 2. The highlighted green rows indicate a positive variation in the elderly individuals' feelings of loneliness. This improvement was observed six times, representing 50% of the sample. For 5 people (41.7%), their perception remained the same. These individuals had already reported feeling "quite accompanied," indicating that they did not experience feelings of loneliness or social isolation. Only one individual experienced a negative change after using the system, transitioning from "somewhat accompanied" to feeling "quite alone".

Table 2. Evolution of the perception of loneliness/social isolation

Participants	Age	Before tests	After tests
1	73	Quite accompanied	Quite accompanied
2	78	Quite accompanied	Quite accompanied
3	83	Quite accompanied	Fully accompanied
4	77	Quite alone	Something alone
5	77	Something alone	Neither alone nor accompanied
6	58	Quite accompanied	Fully accompanied
7	80	Quite accompanied	Quite accompanied
8	62	Quite accompanied	Fully accompanied
9	82	Quite accompanied	Quite accompanied
10	85	Neither alone nor accompanied	Something accompanied
11	58	Something accompanied	Something alone
12	76	Quite accompanied	Quite accompanied

Regarding the acceptance of the proposed system, 16.7% (2 individuals) expressed a high level of interest in continuing to receive notifications on television. Half of the sample, 6 participants, stated that they have an interest in the solution. However, 2 individuals mentioned that they are not interested in continuing to use the proposed technology. Only 1 individual (8.3%) expressed little interest.

Specifically regarding the device, participants were asked if they would like to receive the notifications on another device. Only 2 individuals (16.7%) mentioned that they would prefer to receive them on their cell phones. Eight (66.7%) chose the option "TV shared by more people," and 2 (16.7%) opted for "TV for more personal use". This indicates that television is indeed a suitable device for receiving this type of content.

Finally, regarding the most appropriate times, the participants' preferred period, according to their opinion, is between the afternoon and the early evening (12 PM to 7 PM). It is also worth mentioning that, although it was not the objective of the study, questions related to the usability of the system were asked. Eight individuals (66.8%) mentioned that they received the notifications on televisions considered "average," and four chose the option "on large televisions, above 50 inches". Regarding the ease of reading, 10 people (83.3%) found the notifications "adequate," and 2 people found them "inadequate". Regarding the interference caused by the notifications in the display of content, 8 individuals (66.7%) stated that it was "adequate," 3 (25%) considered it "very adequate," and only 1 person (8.7%) found it "inadequate".

4   Conclusions and Future Work

This paper belongs to a larger study that has gone through different phases before reaching this stage. Firstly, a systematic review was conducted to detect related studies [19]. Next, 20 elderly individuals were interviewed to identify their opinions on the subject [19]. Finally, as mentioned earlier, a focus group was conducted with the target audience, followed by a field test with 12 individuals.

The results obtained from the focus group and field test clearly demonstrate that the older adults are not indifferent to the proposed solution. Sending notifications to the TV captured their attention and had an impact on their daily routines.

Specifically, during the focus group session, the participants showed a positive acceptance of the presented scenarios and were receptive to television notifications. They spontaneously expressed that receiving messages via television would be easier for them due to their familiarity with the device and the larger screen, which facilitates content visualization. They believed that this simpler mechanism would allow them to maintain better contact with family and friends through different formats such as text messages and video calls. This perception indicates that senior citizens are open to using the television as a means of communication, and this type of interaction has great potential to enhance intergenerational communication, effectively mitigating social isolation and loneliness that are prevalent among this population.

The field test further confirmed this perception, involving 12 senior individuals over a 44-day period. Notifications regarding birthdays and local events generally made participants feel closer to their families and communities. In terms of notifications that prompted phone calls, most participants actually made the suggested calls, highlighting the potential of such messages to promote intergenerational connections.

Considering that older individuals spend a considerable amount of time watching television, with some participants reporting watching for more than 6 h a day, the likelihood of being impacted by notifications increases. Consequently, they are consistently reminded to call and congratulate their family members, as well as participate in community events. As previous research has shown [23, 24], this kind of stimulus is crucial for the development and improvement of memory-related aspects in older adults.

Based on this perspective and the results gathered in the study, it was made clear that notifications have significant potential to encourage the use of technological resources that facilitate connections between different generations.

To further explore this topic, the next step is to integrate an intelligent virtual assistant into the proposed notification system. The aim is to enable the older adults to perform the tasks suggested in the notifications using voice commands. By utilizing spoken commands, making calls, and sending messages would become easier without the need for typing or accessing applications. This comprehensive system will be tested with another group of older adults in a real-life context, and the results will be published in future papers.

Acknowledgements. This work is funded by National Funds through the FCT - Fundação para a Ciência e Tecnologia.

References

1. Who Homepage: Ageing and Health. https://www.who.int/news-room/fact-sheets/detail/ageing-and-health. Accessed 07 Sept 2022
2. UN Homepage. https://www.un.org/en/global-issues/ageing. Accessed 07 Sept 2022
3. Vaportzis, E., Martin, M., Gow, A.J.: A tablet for healthy ageing: the effect of a tablet computer training intervention on cognitive abilities in older adults. Am. J. Geriatr. Psychiatry **25**(8), 841–851 (2017)
4. Rito, F.: You & Me TV – Televisão social para idosos (Doctoral dissertation). Repository of University of Lisboa (2015)
5. Frey, B.S.: Happiness and television viewing. In: Frey, B.S. (ed.) Economics of Happiness. SpringerBriefs in Economics, pp. 51–54. Springer, Cham (2018). https://doi.org/10.1007/978-3-319-75807-7_10
6. GNR Homepage. https://www.gnr.pt/comunicado.aspx?linha=4625. Accessed 07 Sept 2022
7. ICS Homepage. https://www.ics.ulisboa.pt/sites/ics.ulisboa.pt/files/2022/inquerito_praticas_culturais_2020.pdf. Accessed 07 Sept 2022
8. Coelho, J., Rito, F., Duarte, C.: "You, me & TV"—fighting social isolation of older adults with Facebook, TV and multimodality. Int. J. Hum. Comput. Stud. **98**, 8–50 (2017)
9. Voit, A., Weber, D., Stowell, E., Henze, N.: Caloo: an ambient pervasive smart calendar to support aging in place. In: MUM 2017: Proceedings of the 16th International Conference on Mobile and Ubiquitous Multimedia, pp. 25–30. Association for Computing Machinery, New York (2017)
10. Hong, T., Su, Y., Lee, H., Hsieh, C., Chiu, J.: VisualLink: strengthening the connection between hearing-impaired elderly and their family. In: CHI Conference on Human Factors in Computing Systems, pp. 67–73. Association for Computing Machinery, New York (2017)
11. Valtolina, S., Hu, L.: Charlie: a chatbot to improve the elderly quality of life and to make them more active to fight their sense of loneliness. In: CHItaly 2021: 14th Biannual Conference of the Italian SIGCHI Chapter (CHItaly 2021), pp. 1–5. Association for Computing Machinery, New York (2021)

12. Santana-Mancilla, C., Anido-Rifón, E.: iTVCare: a home care system for the elderly through interactive television. In: Proceedings of the Seventh Mexican Conference on Human-Computer Interaction (MexIHC 2018), vol. 1, p. 92 (2018)
13. Glaser, B.G., Strauss, A.L.: The Discovery of Grounded Theory - Strategies for Qualitative Research, 1st edn. Routledge, London (2017)
14. Bardin, L.: Análise de Conteúdo. Edições 70, Lisboa (2011)
15. Hammer, S., et al.: Design of a lifestyle recommender system for the elderly. In: Proceedings of the 8th ACM International Conference on Pervasive Technologies Related to Assistive Environments, pp. 1–8. Association for Computing Machinery, New York (2015)
16. Mainetti, L., Patrono, L., Secco, A., Sergi, I.: An IoT-aware AAL system for elderly people. In: 2016 International Multidisciplinary Conference on Computer and Energy Science, SpliTech 2016, Split, Croatia, pp. 1–6. IEEE (2016)
17. Kotevski, A., Koceska, N., Koceski, S: E-health monitoring system E-health monitoring system. In: Proceedings of the 6 International Conference on Applied Internet and Information Technologies, Bitola, Italy, pp. 259–265 (2016)
18. Ramljak, M.: Smart home medication reminder system. In: 2017 25th International Conference on Software, Telecommunications and Computer Networks, SoftCOM 2017, Split, Croatia, pp. 1–5. IEEE (2017)
19. Camargo, J., Silva, T., Abreu, J.: Connect elderly to other generations through iTV: evaluating notifications' potential. In: Abásolo, M.J., Olmedo Cifuentes, G.F. (eds.) jAUTI 2021. CCIS, vol. 1597, pp. 20–35. Springer, Cham (2022). https://doi.org/10.1007/978-3-031-22210-8_2
20. Hong, T., Su, Y., Lee, H., Hsieh, C., Chiu, J.: VisualLink: strengthening the connection between hearing-impaired elderly and their family. In: Conference on Human Factors in Computing Systems, pp. 67–73 (2017)
21. Santos, R., Beja, J., Rodrigues, M., Martins, C.: Designing visual interfaces to support voice input: the case of a TV application to request help in daily life tasks. In: ACM International Conference Proceeding Series (2019). https://doi.org/10.1145/3335595.3335637
22. Encarnação, J., et al.: A management system to personalize notifications in the TV ecosystem. Procedia Comput. Sci. **219**, 674–679 (2023). https://doi.org/10.1016/j.procs.2023.01.338
23. Small, G.W., et al.: Brain health consequences of digital technology use. Dialogues Clin. Neurosci. **22**(2), 179–187 (2020). https://doi.org/10.31887/DCNS.2020.22.2/gsmall
24. Pradhan, A., Lazar, A., Findlater, L.: Use of intelligent voice assistants by older adults with low technology use. ACM Trans. Comput. Hum. Interact. **27**(4), Article no. 3 (2020). https://doi.org/10.1145/3373759

Digital Infrastructure

Encryption of Messages and Additional Information in Digital Terrestrial Television's Transport Stream Using PSI/SI Tables

Evelina Silva, Nelson Benavides, and Gonzalo Olmedo(⊠)

WiCOM-Energy Research Group, Department of Electrical, Electronic and
Telecommunications, Universidad de las Fuerzas Armadas ESPE, Sangolquí, Ecuador
{mesilva,nbbenavides1,gfolmedo}@espe.edu.ec

Abstract. Digital terrestrial television plays a vital role in emergency support systems by providing a means to transmit additional information to support personnel. This information can be sent through the transport stream using file communication protocols or text, utilizing receivers specifically designed for this purpose. This article proposes an encryption algorithm that operates within the unused spaces of the Program Specific Information/System Information (PSI/SI) tables in the MPEG2-TS standard transport stream. The algorithm ensures that the encryption process does not impact the audio, video, data, or original table configuration. The methodology presented in this article enables secure transmission of encrypted messages while preserving the integrity of the original content.

Keywords: Encryption · TS · TDT · ISDB-T

1 Introduction

Traditionally, the digital terrestrial television signal transmission system under the ISDB-T standard is implemented using a Transport Stream (TS) [1]. The TS comprises packets with a size of 188 bytes [2]. To configure the modulation system remotely, which defines the hierarchical structure of the system through its layers, considering the utilized modulations, channel coding structure, and guard time of the OFDM signal, an additional 16 bytes of information are included. As a result, the packets increase in size to 204 bytes, known as Broadcast Transport Stream (BTS) [3]. These BTS packets contain specific information about both general and specific PSI/SI tables of the ISDB-T standard [4].

To transmit audio, video, and data signals within the TS or BTS file, a fixed bandwidth of 29.958 MHz is allocated. However, since the entire bandwidth is not fully utilized by the video, audio, and data information, it is necessary to pad the TS or BTS with null packets to ensure it reaches the designated bandwidth [5]. Consequently, a TS or BTS file will contain numerous null packets within its structure. It is worth noting that the packets representing the PSI/SI (Program Specific Information/Service Information) tables have a limited size, which is generally smaller than the 188-byte size of a BTS packet. The unused bytes in the packet are filled with the hexadecimal value 0xFF, a common practice found in both TS and BTS packets [5].

© The Author(s), under exclusive license to Springer Nature Switzerland AG 2023
M. J. Abásolo et al. (Eds.): jAUTI 2022, CCIS 1820, pp. 101–113, 2023.
https://doi.org/10.1007/978-3-031-45611-4_7

In addition to these blank spaces, there are reserved bits or spaces available for future implementations. This allows for diverse data transmission methods within a Transport Stream, utilizing these blank spaces efficiently. Moreover, many transport networks strive to reduce bandwidth usage. Consequently, the padding packets can be eliminated, leaving only the essential PSI/SI tables that can be independently structured using generators at the television stations.

Within the ISDB-T standard, the Emergency Broadcasting System (EWBS) can be transmitted. Currently, it is still under development and evaluation for implementation in Ecuador [6, 7]. This system includes an emergency alert area code structure that the transmitter sends. This code triggers the activation of televisions and other set-top-box that have one of these codes configured. The activation of the emergency alert consists of an audible alarm in the case of decoders, as well as the on-screen presentation of the sent emergency alert text message through superimposition.

The TS structure allows for diverse transmission of data, as the digitization of video and audio enables their combination with other data types. This includes carrying basic information such as program guides, interactive application data, emergency alerts, parental controls, among others, which are typically part of the programming. Furthermore, this concept can be expanded to transmit data that can be decoded by specialized equipment, providing support to fire, police, or military teams engaged in emergency response operations. Thus, the first option would be to transmit the data through standardized communication protocols like Digital Storage Media Command and Control (DSM-CC) [8]. Alternatively, encrypting the information within the audio, video, or PSI/SI tables could be considered. The Program Association Tables (PAT) and Program Map Tables (PMT), which are always present, can incorporate encryption of information within the packets containing PAT and PMT tables. By modifying the null bytes, it becomes possible to transmit enhanced emergency information within the TS or BTS packets. This approach aims to facilitate support during emergencies and allow for better visualization of the decrypted report.

This article is structured as follows: Sect. 2 introduces the proposed methodology for encrypting and decrypting information within the blank spaces of the PSI tables. Section 3 presents the results obtained from the implementation of the methodology. Finally, Sect. 4 provides the concluding remarks and summarizes the key findings of the study.

2 Methodology

Based on the mentioned information in the introduction section, there are several ways to transmit additional data within the structure of a TS to contribute to new types of services that can be exclusively read by receivers designed for this purpose. This article presents a proposal based on including encrypted messages within the PSI tables, specifically the Program Association Table (PAT) and Program Map Table (PMT). These tables are constant throughout the transmission stages, as they define the programming to be sent, and their configuration can be structured to remain consistent throughout the entire transmission chain, including both streaming and digital television transmission.

In the context of working with the PSI tables, the initial phase involves conducting an analysis of the PAT and PMT tables. This analysis encompasses the calculation of the available space that can be utilized and the determination of the number of packets being transmitted. Considering the periodic retransmission of these tables every 100 ms and their ability to accommodate coordinated information, a calculation is performed to ascertain the available space within these tables. Upon completion of this analysis, the transmission algorithm for the data structure, which will serve as a container for the desired files to be transmitted, is proposed. This algorithm adheres to the general structure illustrated in Fig. 1.

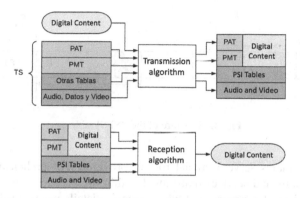

Fig. 1. Proposed Block Diagram of Encryption Algorithms.

After developing the transmission algorithm, the decryption algorithm is proposed to retrieve the information from the encrypted data. Finally, a laboratory test will be conducted to validate the proposed methodology. A controlled scenario has been defined, where the encrypted signal will be transmitted over the air, and then the captured signal will be analyzed. By reading the TS and using the decryption algorithm, the information will be recovered and validated.

The laboratory test aims to evaluate the effectiveness and accuracy of the proposed methodology under controlled conditions. By transmitting the encrypted information over the air and subsequently capturing and processing the signal, the decryption algorithm will be applied to retrieve the information successfully. The results obtained from this test will provide valuable insights into the feasibility and reliability of the proposed methodology for transmitting encrypted messages within the PSI tables of a TS.

In summary, this methodology involves analyzing the PAT and PMT tables, developing a transmission algorithm for the data structure, proposing a decryption algorithm, and conducting a laboratory test to validate the proposed methodology. By implementing this methodology, it is expected to enable the secure transmission of additional information within the PSI tables, contributing to the advancement of new services and enhancing the capabilities of receivers designed to interpret and utilize this encrypted data.

2.1 Transmission Algorithm

In the transmission algorithm, a TS file is selected in read mode, with the file extension ".TS," to access essential information about the file's elements, such as its name and the size of bytes it contains. By dividing the file size by 188, the number of packets within the file's structure can be determined. Each packet comprising the TS file is then analyzed, specifically targeting the PAT and PMT. These tables are located based on their PID (Packet Identifier).

Upon locating the PAT and PMT tables, the algorithm proceeds to access the content of a digital file to be inserted into these tables. It is crucial to consider the structure of the PSI/SI Tables while performing this activity, as depicted in Fig. 2.

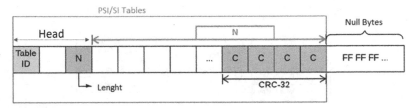

Fig. 2. Structure of the PSI/SI tables.

The PSI/SI Tables serve a crucial role in providing comprehensive information about the programs and services transmitted within the TS file. These tables encompass vital metadata, descriptors, and other essential details necessary for receivers to accurately interpret and process the transmitted data. To ensure the seamless integration of encrypted messages, the transmission algorithm follows the established format and protocols, appropriately incorporating them into the PSI/SI Tables.

This step of the methodology necessitates precise analysis and manipulation of the PSI/SI Tables. Any errors or inconsistencies in this process could have adverse effects on the compatibility and interpretability of the transmitted data by receivers. Thus, it is imperative to ensure the seamless integration of encrypted messages within the PSI/SI Tables while preserving the integrity and functionality of the existing information.

By adhering to the defined structure of the PSI/SI Tables and carefully inserting the encrypted content within the PAT and PMT tables, the transmission algorithm enables the secure transmission of additional information alongside the regular programming. This expanded methodology encompasses the intricate processes of accessing, analyzing, and modifying the PSI/SI Tables to effectively incorporate encrypted messages. By doing so, it enhances the capabilities and versatility of the TS file transmission system.

Moreover, the PSI/SI tables are identifiable through their respective packet identification, which distinguishes the content contained within each packet. The length of information carried by each packet is displayed, and any remaining space is filled with null bytes, denoted by the hexadecimal value 0xFF. It is within these spaces that the encrypted information will be inserted into the PAT and PMT tables. In the subsequent section, the structure of the PAT and PMT tables will be presented in detail.

The payload, depicted within the green lines in Fig. 2, represents the information presented in Figs. 3 and 4. This payload has a total size of 184 bytes. Preceding the payload is the packet header, which spans 4 bytes. Once the payload is complete, the remaining bytes are filled with null bytes, represented by the hexadecimal value 0xFF, amounting to a total of 184 bytes. It is within these null bytes that the information of the digital content is inserted.

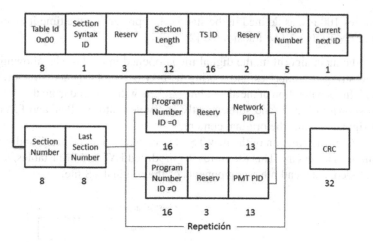

Fig. 3. Structure of the PAT table.

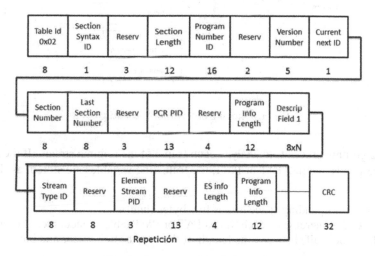

Fig. 4. Structure of the PMT table.

Calculating the size of the digital file, denoted by η, as a function of the TS file's duration time (t_{TS}) and the padding bytes available between the PMT and PAT tables, the following equation is utilized:

$$\eta = \frac{xt_{TS}}{3t_t}, \tag{1}$$

where:

- η, represents the size of the file to be encrypted, expressed in bytes.
- t_{TS}, corresponds to the duration time of the TS.
- x, denotes the number of available padding bytes combined across the PAT and PMT tables.
- t_t, signifies 100 ms, as defined in the standard, representing the time it takes for the PAT and PMT tables to be transmitted [2].

Within the main algorithm, the digital file is opened in read mode, allowing access to the byte string it comprises and storing it in two vectors named "vectordig" and "voriginal". In each iteration of the algorithm, packets will be sliced from the "vectordig" vector, as shown in Fig. 5, and subsequently encrypted into the PAT and PMT tables, while "voriginal" retains the original content.

Additionally, the creation of the new TS file, named "TS_encript.ts," and opening it in write mode is necessary. This file stores the modified PAT and PMT tables, as well as the audio, video, data, and other components of the original TS file.

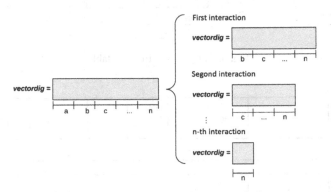

Fig. 5. Clipping process for "vectordig".

The algorithm proceeds to analyze each frame of the original stream. If the frame's PID corresponds to either PAT or PMT, the following variables are stored, as shown in Fig. 6:

1. The amount of padding space minus five bytes (bnul).
2. A counter that increments each time a PAT or PMT table is encountered (cont).
3. The difference (dif) between the length of the "vectordig" vector and bnul.

Subsequently, the byte string of the digital file is accessed, and the insertion of null bytes into the PAT and PMT tables is performed. To accomplish this, the following algorithm is proposed: Insert a 5-byte digital content header into the PAT and PMT tables. The first 3 bytes of the header indicate the packet number, while the remaining 2 bytes are divided into 14 bits allocated for the packet size and two flag bits, as outlined in Table 1.

The primary purpose of this digital content header is to facilitate the decryption process for the receiver. It ensures that the receiver can execute the decryption procedure until all the packets have been recovered, guaranteeing the complete reconstruction of the digital content.

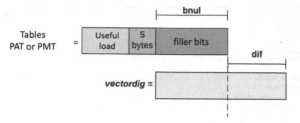

Fig. 6. Variables stored from each PAT or PMT table.

Table 1. Indicator flag bits.

Valor	Indicator
10	Start
00	Transmission
01	End

The header enables the receiver to execute the decryption process until all the packets have been recovered, that is, until the digital content has been reconstructed. The function, as shown in Fig. 7, takes as inputs the mentioned table characteristics (bnul, cont, and dif) and returns the corresponding header as a 5-byte vector called "cab." It also provides a variable called "flag," which defaults to 0 and only changes its value to 1 to indicate that the last packet of digital content should be encrypted in the table.

The first step performed by the function is to convert the number "cont" into three bytes, which indicate the packet number attached to the table and are placed at the beginning of the header.

The next process involves checking the value of "dif." If "dif" is greater than or equal to zero, it indicates that the packet's length will occupy all the null bytes in the table, and the value of the "flag" is set to 0. On the other hand, if "dif" is less than zero, it signifies that the packet will not occupy all the null bytes, and therefore, the packet size will be equal to the length of the "vectordig," and the value of the "flag" changes to 1.

The length of the corresponding packet is converted into a 14-bit string and concatenated with the 2-bit indicator specified in Table 1, forming the final two bytes of the header.

Following the insertion of the header, the byte string is incorporated into the null bytes of the PAT and PMT tables, as depicted in Fig. 8. Once this process is complete, a new TS file is generated, containing the encrypted information and ready for transmission.

2.2 Reception Algorithm

The process begins by opening the TS file and retrieving information about the number of bytes and packets it contains. Subsequently, the PIDs of the PAT table and the PMT table are searched to locate the digital content package. To facilitate this analysis, a function called ANALYSIS is created, which examines the 5-byte header vector of the

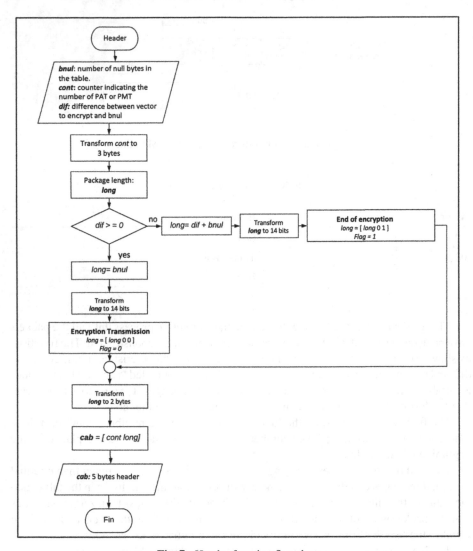

Fig. 7. Header function flowchart.

digital file. This header indicates whether the packet contains the end-of-digital-content information.

The reconstruction of the digital content involves two scenarios. In the first case, the reception starts from the beginning of the transmission, while in the second case, the reception begins from an unknown moment, resulting in the final packet being found before the first one.

To address these variations, the received file is opened and stored in a variable named TRAMA within the PAT and PMT tables, resolving these potential inconsistencies. By utilizing the ANALYSIS function, it is possible to determine when the digital content restarts, allowing for correct decryption and ensuring the file is reconstructed in the

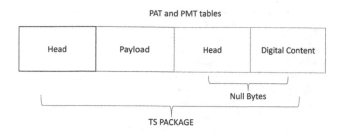

Fig. 8. Structure of the PAT and PMT tables with the encrypted message.

appropriate order. Finally, the decrypted file is created, enabling its visualization and comparison with the original file.

3 Results

Once the encrypted TS file has been generated, the transmission and reception of the signal are carried out. For this purpose, the DEKTEC DTA-115 modulating card and the Stream Xpress software are employed for the transmission process, while the RANGER NEO 2 equipment receives the TS file via an antenna. The received signal is then captured and stored for further analysis. Once the transmission is completed, the TS file is copied for research purposes.

The first step involves analyzing the encrypted TS file and verifying the transmitted information using a TS and BTS analyzer. The configuration for this analysis is depicted in Fig. 9, which illustrates the encryption of an image in the PAT table, and Fig. 10, which demonstrates the encryption of the image in the PMT table.

To locate each table, the search engine is populated with the value of 0 for the PAT table and the value of 4096 for the PMT table. These values are inserted, as shown in Figs. 9 and 10, respectively. In the figures, the light blue box represents the header of the encrypted data, while the purple box contains the bytes of the digital content.

Upon obtaining the new TS file from the RANGER NEO 2 equipment, its content is examined using a TS and BTS analyzer. However, the order of the content may differ from the original transmission. To address this, the ANALYSIS function and MATLAB software are utilized to organize the content. A variable is employed to store the encrypted file, ensuring smooth decryption. Once this step is completed, the content of the packets within the PAT and PMT tables is displayed, as illustrated in Fig. 11 and Fig. 12, respectively.

Figures 11 and 12 present the outcome of organizing the received signal using an undetermined order vector. To facilitate the ordering process and display the transmitted image, the image is transmitted three times within the PAT and PMT tables. This allows for locating the start of the digital data and arranging it in the vector accordingly.

When transmitting the image, it is important to note that the original audio and video signal remains unaltered, ensuring optimal reception performance. Moreover, the encrypted image can be visualized in a file generated from a MATLAB picture, as depicted in Fig. 13.

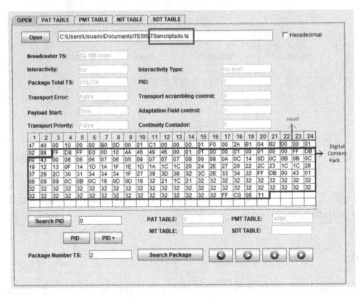

Fig. 9. Structure of the PAT table with the encrypted message.

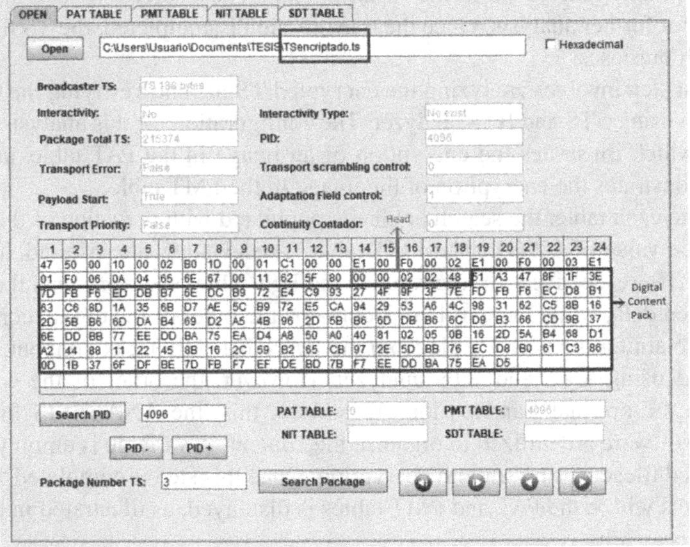

Fig. 10. Structure of the PMT table with the encrypted message.

Figure 13 is the result of transmitting an encrypted and decrypted image in the null bytes of the PAT and PMT Tables. In the same way, any digital information that is necessary to information can be sent, as is the case of early emergency alerts that, by encrypting the data, can be sent more quickly to the population.

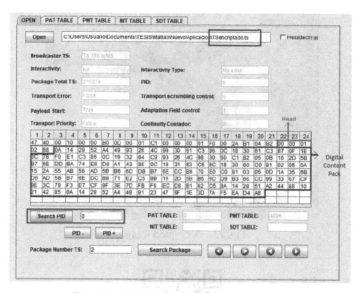

Fig. 11. PAT table with vector content pack.

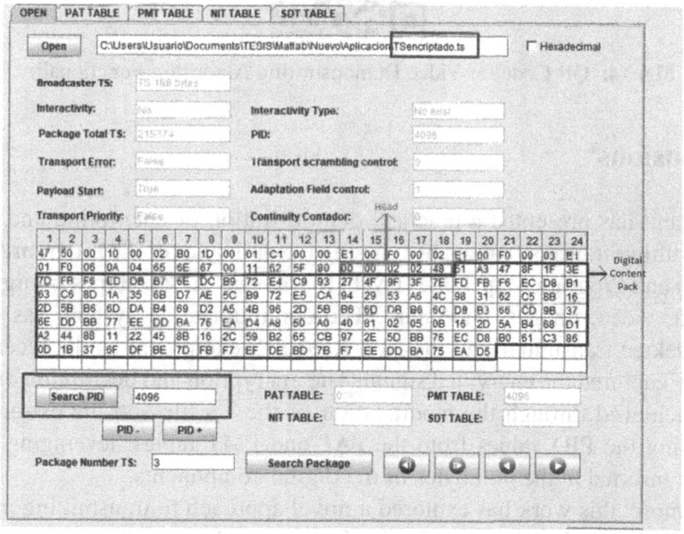

Fig. 12. PMT table with vector content pack.

The practical demonstration of the results presented in this section can be viewed through a video available at the following link https://youtu.be/6Z4HRPnbAGw. Additionally, access to the video can be obtained using the QR code provided in Fig. 14.

Fig. 13. Decrypted image.

Fig. 14. QR Code for Video Demonstrating Algorithm Functionality.

4   Conclusions

This document has presented a practical demonstration of encrypting and decrypting messages within a transport stream by utilizing the null bytes of the Program Association Table (PAT) and Program Map Table (PMT) to transmit various types of digital content such as text, video, images, and audio. The communication system was established using the Dektec transmitter and the Neo Ranger 2 equipment as the receiver, which successfully captured the encrypted signal. The encryption and decryption of the digital data were achieved through the modification of the TS file and the extraction of the message using the PID values from the PAT and PMT tables, leveraging the header information inserted in the null bytes of the digital components.

Furthermore, this work has explored a novel approach to transmitting information, including emergency data, in a communication system that may remain imperceptible to the user, but can be effectively utilized by compatible receivers to deliver early warning alerts during emergencies.

The primary focus of this research is on utilizing null bytes to transmit additional information and make efficient use of the channel bandwidth. By incorporating encrypted messages within the PSI tables, specifically the PAT and PMT, new types of services can be developed that can be exclusively accessed by receivers designed for this purpose. This article has proposed a methodology based on this concept, taking into account the constant nature of these tables throughout the transmission stages and their ability to accommodate coordinated information, ensuring consistency in the transmission chain, including both streaming and digital television broadcast.

The proposed methodology involves analyzing the PAT and PMT tables, determining the available space for additional data, designing a transmission algorithm for the data structure, developing a decryption algorithm to retrieve the encrypted information, and conducting a laboratory test to validate the effectiveness and reliability of the proposed methodology. The controlled laboratory test will involve transmitting the encrypted signal over the air and analyzing the captured signal, applying the decryption algorithm to successfully recover and validate the information.

The laboratory test aims to evaluate the feasibility and accuracy of the proposed methodology under controlled conditions. By successfully transmitting and decrypting the encrypted information, the results of this test will provide valuable insights into the potential of the proposed methodology for securely transmitting encrypted messages within the PSI tables of a transport stream.

In conclusion, this methodology offers a comprehensive approach to securely transmit additional information within PSI tables, thereby advancing new services and enhancing the capabilities of receivers designed to interpret and utilize this encrypted data. The successful implementation of this methodology will contribute to the development of secure and efficient communication systems in various domains.

References

1. Uehara, M.: Application of MPEG-2 systems to terrestrial ISDB (ISDB-T). Proc. IEEE **94**(1), 261–268 (2006). https://doi.org/10.1109/JPROC.2005.859695
2. Villamarín, D., Olmedo, G., Lara, R., Illescas, M.A.: Generación de Transport Stream con Audio, Video y Datos de Interactividad para el Sistema de Televisión Digital Terrestre ISDB-Tb. MASKAY **2**(1), 49–55 (2012)
3. Akamine, C., Iano, Y., de Melo Valeira, G., Bedicks, G.: Re-multiplexing ISDB T BTS into DVB TS for SFN. IEEE Trans. Broadcast. **55**(4), 802–809 (2009). https://doi.org/10.1109/TBC.2009.2032796
4. Pisciotta, N., Liendo, C., Lauro, R.: Trasmisión de Televisión Digital Terrestre en la Norma ISDB-Tb. Universidad Blas Pascal. CENGAGE Learning, 1ª edn. (2013). ISBN 978-987-1954-08-7
5. El-Hajjar, M., Hanzo, L.: A survey of digital television broadcast transmission techniques. IEEE Commun. Surv. Tutor. **15**(4), 1924–1949 (2013). Fourth Quarter. https://doi.org/10.1109/SURV.2013.030713.00220
6. Olmedo, G., Acosta, F., Haro, R., Villamarín, D., Benavides, N.: Broadcast testing of emergency alert system for digital terrestrial television EWBS in ecuador. In: Abásolo, M., Silva, T., González, N. (eds.) jAUTI 2018. CCIS, vol. 1004, pp. 176–187. Springer, Cham (2019). https://doi.org/10.1007/978-3-030-23862-9_13
7. Olmedo, G., Acosta, F., Villamarín, D., Santander, F., Achig, R., Morocho, V.: Prototype of a centralized alert and emergency system for digital terrestrial television in ecuador. In: Botto-Tobar, M., Cruz, H., Díaz Cadena, A. (eds.) CIT 2020. AISC, vol. 1326, pp. 191–201. Springer, Cham (2021). https://doi.org/10.1007/978-3-030-68080-0_14
8. Lee, N., Chae, S., Lee, H., Kim, H.: Cooperation system of DSM-CC data carousel and MPEG-4 system via satellite. In: Proceedings. International Conference on Information Technology: Coding and Computing, Las Vegas, NV, USA, pp. 421–424 (2002). https://doi.org/10.1109/ITCC.2002.1000426

On Using a Microearthquake Recognition System for an Early Warning System at Cotopaxi Volcano

Román Lara[1]([✉]) [iD], Santiago Altamirano[1] [iD], Julio Larco[1] [iD], Diego Benítez[2] [iD], and Noel Pérez[2] [iD]

[1] WiCOM-Energy Research Group, Centro de Investigación de Redes Ad Hoc, Universidad de las Fuerzas Armadas – ESPE, Sangolquí, Ecuador
`{ralara,bsaltamirano,jclarco}@espe.edu.ec`
[2] Colegio de Ciencias e Ingenierías, Universidad San Francisco de Quito, Quito, Ecuador
`{dbenitez,nperez}@usfq.edu.ec`

Abstract. Volcanic activity has been increasing throughout the world, posing a significant threat to populations in the event of eruptions. Ecuador, which hosts several active volcanoes, requires robust methods for identifying potential eruptions and issuing reliable alerts to protect lives and minimize damages. This paper presents the development of an automatic microseism recognition system integrated with the Early Warning Broadcast System (EWBS). Using models such as k-Nearest Neighbors, Support Vector Machine, and Decision Trees, along with frequency-based features extracted from seismic data provided by the Instituto Geofísico de la Escuela Politécnica Nacional, the recognition system aims to accurately detect and classify microeartquakes associated with the Cotopaxi volcano during 2012. During the detection stage, the system achieves an impressive Balanced Error Rate (BER) of 0.01, indicating its effectiveness in identifying events. In the subsequent classification stage, the system achieves a BER of 0.11, demonstrating its ability to classify events accurately. The classifiers were further evaluated using 82 microearthquakes, comprising 41 LP events and 41 VT events, resulting in an accuracy of 85% and a BER of 0.15. In addition, a larger data set of 563 earthquakes, consisting of 522 LP events and 41 VT events, was used to assess the performance of the classifiers. The results showed a 7% increase in accuracy compared to the previous test, demonstrating improved performance. However, 11 earthquakes were still misclassified. Integration of these classifiers with a voting system improves their performance. The selected set of 50 features plays a crucial role in achieving accurate results. The recognition system seamlessly interfaces with the EWBS, ensuring a 30 s delay before launching an early warning. This delay provides valuable time for preparation and response measures. In conclusion, the developed microearthquake recognition system, combined with the EWBS, demonstrates its effectiveness in detecting and classifying events, thereby enhancing the ability to issue timely and reliable alerts for volcanic activity. The findings contribute to improved volcano monitoring and risk mitigation strategies.

Keywords: EWBS · ISDB-T · Recognition system · TDT

M. J. Abásolo et al. (Eds.): jAUTI 2022, CCIS 1820, pp. 114–128, 2023.
https://doi.org/10.1007/978-3-031-45611-4_8

1 Introduction

Early warning systems have proven to be an effective source for protecting lives against possible natural disasters such as landslides [1], floods [2], tsunamis [3, 4], although there is a major gap for earthquakes [5, 6] and volcanic eruptions [7]. The latter represent one of the constantly looming natural hazards that threaten the balance of ecosystems; in such a sense, vulcanologists are constantly monitoring volcanoes, in order to identify characteristics related to soil deformation, gas flow, seismicity, and other factors, which allow one to alert society effectively. In this sense, there exist some early warning broadcast systems (EWBS) deployed around the world, with the aim of providing alerts and warnings related to volcanic activity. Some examples include the Volcano Notification Service in the United States, which uses a combination of seismometers, gas sensors, and satellite imagery to detect and monitor volcanic activity [8], the Global Disaster Alert and Coordination System in the European Union, this system provides real-time information on natural disasters, including volcanic eruptions, to support humanitarian response efforts [9], the Volcano Alert Level System in New Zealand, the system assigns alert levels to volcanoes based on their current activity, ranging from 0 (no volcanic unrest) to 5 (major volcanic eruption in progress) [10], and the Volcano Early Warning and Monitoring System in the Philippines, in which, the system provides early warning alerts for volcanic hazards such as ashfall, lava flow, and pyroclastic flows through a network of monitoring stations and real-time data analysis [11]. These systems play a key role in minimizing the potential impact of volcanic eruptions and ensuring the safety of communities near active volcanoes, in which information is collected from various sources and distributed by media, including websites, email alerts, social networks, SMS, radio, and television.

In this context, seismology is an important tool for recognizing changes in volcanoes. Around the world, the institutions responsible for volcanic surveillance in conjunction with their expert analysts [12–14], who can interpret the seismic signature to recognize different types of microearthquakes that can occur [15] and based on this information, recommend the launch or change of an early warning issued by the relevant entities [16]. In the case of Ecuador, which is considered one of the countries with many active volcanoes around the world, as it is located in the Pacific Ring of Fire, where there are permanent volcanic and seismic activities [17], the Geophysical Institute of the National Polytechnic School (IGEPN, from the spanish, *Instituto Geofísico de la Escuela Politécnica Nacional*) has been responsible for seismic and volcanic monitoring. In addition, the IGEPN is the entity responsible for recommending to the Secretariat for Risk Management (SGR, from the spanish, *Secretaría de Gestión de Riesgos*) to issue timely and effective alert changes to the community, with possible impact, in order to follow the recommendations provided by it. Currently, there are several volcanoes in an eruptive process: Tungurahua, Reventador, Sangay, Chiles, and Cotopaxi. The latter is one of the most dangerous volcanoes as it can affect around 300,000 inhabitants in case of an eruption. For this reason, a monitoring system has been deployed and a seismic analysis is used to recommend an alert change [18]. Therefore, using the EWBS based on the terrestrial digital television system in accordance with the Integrated Services Digital Broadcasting-Terrestrial (ISDB-T) standard for issuing timely alerts, becomes a necessary alternative.

For these reasons, the aim of this paper is to develop an early warning system for a potential eruption of the Cotopaxi volcano based on the increase of its microearthquakes. To achieve this goal, an automatic recognition system (detection + classification) of microearthquakes is proposed, by considering traditional machine learning techniques such as support vector machines (SVM), k-nearest neighbors (k-NN) and decision trees (DT). Performance evaluation of recognition systems is carried out in terms of accuracy (A), precision (P), sensitivity (S), specificity, or recall (R) and balanced error rate (Ber). For the Ber, the IGEPN requires it to be less than or equal to 0.01 in detection and classification. To improve performance metrics, a voting system is used among the developed systems. Finally, the EWBS system is deployed on a low-cost card, by which an early warning is issued by activating the EWBS system based on ISDB-T. The definition of incremental ranges of the number of microearthquakes related to the different alerts defined in the Ecuadorian state is beyond the scope of this paper.

The rest of the paper is organized as follows. In Sect. 2, we describe the methods and materials used for system design and evaluation. Section 3 presents the experimentation process and how the results were obtained for the detection, classification, and emergency launch stages. Finally, our conclusion and future work are presented in Sect. 4.

2 Methodology

The early warning system for the Cotopaxi volcano consists of several interconnected components. Figure 1 shows a high-level block diagram description.

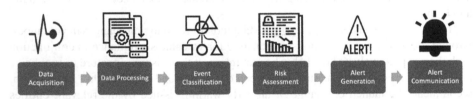

Fig. 1. Block diagram of the proposed early warning system.

Data Acquisition: The first stage consists of the acquisition of seismic and other relevant data from the Cotopaxi volcano. This involves using seismological stations and other sensors distributed near the volcano to monitor its activity. IGEPN has deployed 17 seismological stations on the Cotopaxi volcano. These stations are located on the slopes of the volcano, including five short-period stations (SS) that work in a frequency range of 1 to 50 Hz and 12 broadband stations (BB) that work at a frequency of 0.1 to 50 Hz [19], the deployed network is shown in Fig. 2.

Data Processing: The data collected are processed and analyzed to detect signals from volcanic activity. This involves the application of signal processing techniques and detection algorithms to identify seismic events and other indications of a potential volcanic eruption. For this stage, we propose the use of machine learning techniques; in this sense, three algorithms are used SVM, k-NN, and DT, and we deploy a voting system that is able to maximize performance metrics.

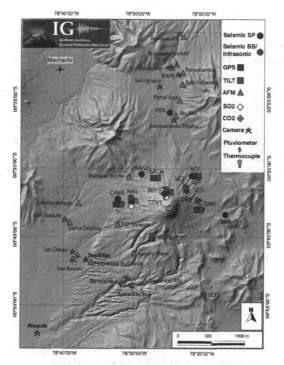

Fig. 2. Network of monitoring stations deployed by IGEPN around the Cotopaxi Volcano.

Event Classification: Once the seismic events are detected, they are classified into different categories, the most frequently occurring microearthquakes are: Long-Period (LP), Volcano-Tectonic (VT), Tremors (TRE), and HYBrids (HYB) [20]. This is achieved by using classification algorithms that use specific event features to assign them a label. For this stage, the same strategy proposed for the detector has been considered.

Risk Assessment: Classified events are evaluated based on their magnitude, location, and other relevant factors to determine the associated risk level. This involves using established models and criteria to assess the potential for a volcanic eruption and its potential impacts. This is beyond the scope of this work.

Alert Generation: Based on the risk assessment, early warnings are generated to inform the authorities and the population near the Cotopaxi volcano about the potential threat. Alerts can include information about the location, estimated magnitude, and safety recommendations. In Ecuador, SNR is the institution in charge of defining this, according to the recommendations given by IGEPN.

Alert Communication: Alerts are communicated through appropriate communication channels such as emergency communication systems, media outlets, mobile applications, and other dissemination channels to reach as many people as possible. At this stage, a prototype of the EWBS is under development with the support of the Japanese government and the Universidad de las Fuerzas Armadas – ESPE.

2.1 Detector

The database used for the detector consists of 350 microearthquakes labeled by experts from IGEPN, including 282 LP, 50 VT, 15 TRE and 3 HYB, and these signals are sorted by month and type of microearthquakes. The signals provided by IGEPN are filtered signals in a range of 1 to 50 Hz, where low-amplitude spikes at frequencies of 0.1 to 0.3 Hz have been previously removed, mainly due to oceanic plate movements. The signals collected by station VC1 are signals with different amplitudes depending on the intensity of each microearthquake, so all signals in the database must be normalized. To perform normalization, the linear trend must be removed and each microearthquake must be scaled to a range of $[-1, 1]$ cantered at zero, for which the following equations are applied:

$$\hat{r}_l = \frac{r_i - \mu_i}{\sigma_i}, \tag{1}$$

where $\hat{r}$ is the normalized signal, μ_i and σ_i are the mean and standard deviation, respectively, and

$$x_i = \frac{\hat{r}_l}{\max|\hat{r}_l|}, \tag{2}$$

where x_i is the signal standardized in a range between $[-1, 1]$. In Fig. 3, a comparison can be seen between an original signal and a normalized one.

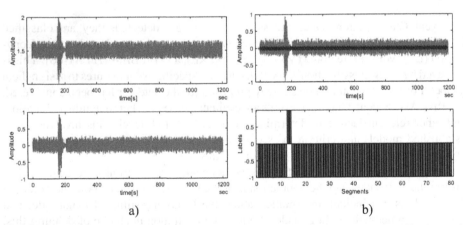

a)   b)

Fig. 3. Example of a record containing a VT event. a) Original record versus normalized record. b) Segmentation and labeling process of a record.

As mentioned before, the database has seismic events with a duration of 20 min, so it is proposed to perform segmentations in time windows. In this work, a segmentation is carried out in 15-s windows, as those carried out in [20], where the best results in the detection of microearthquakes were obtained with different time windows. When performing a 15-s segmentation, 80 segments are obtained for each microearthquake.

These segments are stored in a vector s_i, and finally, each segmented signal is added to a matrix S.

$$s_i = \left[s_{i,1}^T, s_{i,2}^T, s_{i,3}^T, \ldots, s_{i,80}^T \right]^T,$$

where $s_{i,j}$ is a 15-s signal segment of the normalized signal x_i, and conforming

$$S = \left[s_1^T, s_2^T, s_3^T, \ldots, s_M^T \right]^T, \tag{4}$$

where s_M is a vector of each segmented signal, and M is the number of signals in the database. Then, the segments containing the microearthquakes are labeled with $+1$, while the segments without microearthquakes are labeled with -1. This information is included in the database provided by IGEPN. This process is performed for each signal and stored in a vector defined as follows:

$$Y_i = \left[y_{i,1}^T, y_{i,2}^T, y_{i,3}^T, \ldots, y_{i,80}^T \right]^T, \tag{5}$$

where $y_{i,j}$ is the labelling of each segment $s_{i,j}$,

$$Y = \left[Y_1^T, Y_2^T, Y_3^T, \ldots, Y_M^T \right]^T, \tag{6}$$

where Y_M is a vector of each labeled segment, and M is the number of signals in the database. In Fig. 2b, the segmentation and labeling processes can be observed.

Subsequently, the power spectral density (PSD) is calculated for each 15 s segment using the Welch method. The PSD is calculated with a window of 512 points, resulting in a resolution of 257 points. These resolution points are considered as frequency features that are used for training. The PSD of the segmented signal is stored in a matrix W, as follows:

$$w_i = \left[w_{i,1}^T, w_{i,2}^T, w_{i,3}^T, \ldots, w_{i,80}^T \right]^T, \tag{7}$$

where $w_{i,j}$ are the 257 features obtained by using the PSD to each segment $s_{i,j}$,

$$W = \left[w_1^T, w_2^T, w_3^T, \ldots, w_M^T \right]^T, \tag{8}$$

where W_M is the PSD of each extracted signal and M is the number of signals in the database. Finally, with the feature matrix W and the labels Y, we proceed to perform event detection based on supervised learning. For this purpose, various traditional statistical learning methods such as k-NN, DT, and SVM are evaluated. For each classifier, feature selection methods, such as filters, embedded methods, and wrapper methods, are employed, respectively. These methods are evaluated and optimized based on the main performance metrics of the classifier, including A, P, S, R, and Ber. This strategy aims to maximize the probability of identifying segments that contain the majority of microearthquakes.

2.2 Classifier

For this stage, the database used to obtain the classification models was compiled over the years 2012, 2013, 2014, and 2015. This database consists of a total of 1184 microearthquakes with different time variations. It is composed of 1044 LP events, 101 VT events, 27 regional events, 8 HYB events, and 7 glacier rupture events (ICQ, Icequake). The signals have been filtered in the range of 1 to 50 Hz, and the normalization process is carried out by removing the linear trend and scaling each signal to a range of $[-1, 1]$ centered at zero, using Eqs. (1) and (2). For the labeling of the signals, the 1044 LP and the 101 VT were considered. Only these two types of events are used to obtain training models for the classification stage. A label of -1 is assigned to LP events and a label of $+1$ is assigned to VT events. In the feature extraction stage, the PSD is calculated exclusively for microearthquakes using the Welch method and stored in a vector as shown in Eq. (7). PSD is calculated using a window of 512 points, resulting in a resolution of 257 points, which are considered as frequency features. These features are used to train the classifier. The PSD of the signal is stored in a matrix according to Eq. (8). Finally, with the feature matrix W and the microseism label Y, we perform classification by evaluating k-NN, DT, and SVM. For each classifier, feature selection methods, such as filters, embedded methods, and wrapper methods, are employed, respectively. These methods are evaluated and optimized based on the main performance metrics of the classifier, including A, P, S, R, and Ber. This strategy aims to obtain a highly reliable classifier. To improve the performance of the detector and classifier, a voting system is implemented in each stage, where the majority wins. In the detector, the voting system determines whether a segment is part of an event or not, while in the classifier, the voting system mostly determines whether it is a VT or LP event.

2.3 Emergency Alert System

The process of implementing the EWBS in Ecuador involves several steps and considerations. In Fig. 4 shows a block diagram of the process.

Fig. 4. Block diagram of the process to consider a set up for early warning system.

Planning and Collaboration: The implementation of the EWBS requires close collaboration between the Universidad de las Fuerzas Armadas - ESPE, the Ministry of Telecommunications, and other relevant government agencies. A clear plan is developed, outlining the objectives, scope, and timeline of the project.

System Requirements and Design: The technical requirements of the EWBS system are identified, considering factors such as the broadcasting standard used in

Ecuador (ISDB-T), hardware and software components, network infrastructure, and data transmission protocols. The system design is developed accordingly to meet these requirements.

Hardware and Software Setup: The necessary hardware components, such as the ADALM-PLUTO SDR receiver, are procured and installed. The software components, including the necessary drivers and applications, are configured on the designated systems.

Testing and Evaluation: Extensive testing is conducted to ensure the proper functioning of the EWBS system. This includes testing the receiver's ability to capture and analyze the ISDB-T broadcast signal, decoding the alert messages, and transmitting them through the internal network. The system's performance is evaluated based on factors such as response time, message delivery accuracy, and overall reliability.

Integration with Alert Generation: The EWBS system is integrated with the alert generation process, where IGEPN and SGR provide the necessary alert information for volcanic eruptions or other natural disasters. The system is configured to receive and process these alerts, triggering the appropriate warning messages for dissemination.

Communication and Public Awareness: A comprehensive communication strategy is implemented to raise public awareness about the EWBS and its purpose. Educational campaigns are conducted to inform the population about the importance of early warnings, evacuation procedures, and how to respond to the alert messages received through the EWBS.

2.4 Performance

As we mentioned before, in order to evaluate the performance evaluation of the recognition system, in both the detection and the classification performance were measured in terms of:

$$A(\%) = \frac{N_C}{N_T} \times 100, \tag{9}$$

$$P(\%) = \frac{N_{TP}}{N_{TP} + N_{FP}} \times 100, \tag{10}$$

$$R(\%) = \frac{N_{TP}}{N_{TP} + N_{FN}} \times 100, \tag{11}$$

$$S(\%) = \frac{N_{TN}}{N_{TN} + N_{FP}} \times 100, \tag{12}$$

$$Ber = 1 - \frac{R + S}{2 \times 100}, \tag{13}$$

where N_C is the number of correctly classified events, N_T is the total number of events used to feed the classifier, N_{TP} is the number of true positives, N_{FN} is the number of false negatives, N_{TN} is the number of true negatives, and N_{FP} is the number of false positives. We calculated these performance measures using training and testing folds. The time consumption to launch an early warning is denoted by t_p.

3 Results

3.1 Detector Results

By applying the strategies defined in the previous section, the classifier models were obtained with a 60/40 split for training and testing, respectively. For k-NN, the value of k is set to 35, the DT with a 10-fold cross-validation, and the SVM model with ν is set to 0.5. The best features using Mutual Information (MI), Maximum Entropy (ME) and Recursive Feature Elimination (RFE) are identified as 33 of the 257 features considered optimal for all three defined classifiers. This selection helps prevent overfitting. In our case, since we are using frequency-based features, these 33 features correspond to frequency bands that allow distinguishing microseisms from background noise. The relevance order of these features can be observed in Table 1.

Table 1. Identified features with k-NN, DT, and SVM in relevance order in detection stage.

Feature	Frequency (Hz)	Feature	Frequency (Hz)	Feature	Frequency (Hz)
22	4,3	47	9,1	18	3,5
15	2,9	49	9,5	36	7,0
25	4,9	51	9,9	24	4,7
19	3,7	26	5,1	46	8,9
32	6,2	48	9,3	31	6,0
34	6,6	14	2,7	23	4,5
38	7,4	37	7,2	40	7,8
41	8,0	43	8,4	20	3,9
42	8,2	62	12,1	232	45,1
27	5,3	39	7,6	45	8,8
44	8,6	50	9,7	237	46,1

In Fig. 5, it can be seen that the estimated PSD for segments containing a signal can be easily differentiated from the PSD of the background noise. The frequency bands that the algorithms examine are from 0 to 12 Hz and the 40 Hz band. Additionally, a voting system is applied to maximize performance metrics, achieving a Ber of 0.01. This means that for every 100 events, only 1 goes undetected (Table 2).

3.2 Classifier Results

Once the detector has identified an event, according to the IGEPN recommendation, a portion of 1 segment before and after the number of segments defined by the detector is considered. This can be observed in Fig. 6, in which 2 microearthquakes were detected.

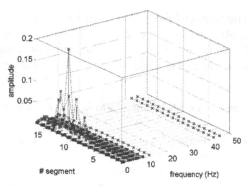

Fig. 5. 20 Examples of segments that contain noise and microearthquakes; the former 10 correspond to the estimated PDF of segments with background noise, and the latter 10 correspond to the estimated PDF of segments that contain part of the microearthquakes.

Table 2. Performance of the detector based on k-NN, DT, SVM classifiers, and a voting system with 33 features.

Algorithm	A (%)	P (%)	R (%)	S (%)	BER
k-NN	98	96	98	98	0,02
DT	79	49	98	74	0,13
SVM	94	85	98	95	0,03
Vote system	**98**	**98**	**99**	**99**	**0,01**

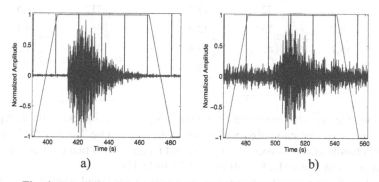

Fig. 6. Examples of 2 events detected. a) VT detected b) LP detected.

After this, we considered a database of 101 VT events, and 101 LP events were randomly selected to work with a balanced data set. The data set was divided into training and testing sets with a 60/40 ratio, resulting in 120 earthquakes (60 LP + 60 VT) for training and model generation, and 82 earthquakes (41 LP + 41 VT) for testing. Furthermore, a final test was conducted using the models obtained, considering 563 earthquakes, with 41 VT and 522 LP events. For k-NN, the value of k was set at 30, DT used 10-fold cross-validation, and the SVM model had ν set to 0.5. The best features, obtained through MI, ME, and RFE, were found to consist of 50 of the 257 features considered optimal for all three classifiers. This selection of features helped prevents overfitting. Table 3 shows the features which allow to discriminate LP from VT.

Table 3. Identified features with k-NN, DT, and SVM in relevance order in classification stage.

Feature	Frequency (Hz)	Feature	Frequency (Hz)	Feature	Frequency (Hz)
17	3,2	50	9,5	75	14,3
19	3,6	44	8,4	77	14,6
16	3,0	46	8,7	74	14,1
18	3,4	86	16,3	87	16,5
20	3,8	39	7,4	42	8,0
21	4,0	38	7,2	47	8,9
15	2,9	81	15,4	84	16,0
22	4,2	79	15,0	82	15,6
14	2,7	43	8,2	68	12,9
13	2,5	11	2,1	78	14,8
12	2,3	85	16,2	35	6,7
23	4,4	76	14,4	31	5,9
24	4,6	51	9,7	27	5,1
49	9,3	72	13,7	71	13,5
45	8,6	73	13,9	36	6,8
80	15,2	41	7,8	40	7,6
30	5,7	48	9,1		

After the feature selection phase, the classifiers produced 50 best features, representing 50 frequencies that maximize performance metrics. Figure 7 shows the frequencies that allow classification between LP and VT, and it can be seen that the frequency bands reviewed are from 2 to 4 Hz, 8 to 10 Hz and 14 to 16 Hz.

The classification results showed an accuracy of 85% and a BER of 0.15 when classifying 82 earthquakes, meaning that 15 out of 100 events were misclassified. When classifying 563 earthquakes, the accuracy improved by 7% and 11 earthquakes were misclassified. The results are presented in Table 4.

3.3 EWBS System Results

The Universidad de las Fuerzas Armadas – ESPE, in collaboration with the Ministry of Telecommunications and the Government of Japan, has developed a system capable of

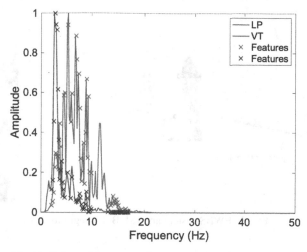

Fig. 7. Selected frequency features to classify LP from VT.

Table 4. Performance of k-NN, DT, SVM classifiers, and voting system with 50 features for 82/563 earthquakes.

Algorithm	A (%)	P (%)	R (%)	S (%)	BER
k-NN	82/93	100/54	63/63	100/96	0,18/0,20
DT	83/87	97/32	68/68	97/89	0,17/0,21
SVM	82/87	84/34	78/78	85/88	0,18/0,17
Voting system	**85/92**	**100/89**	**70/84**	**100/94**	**0,15/0,11**

issuing an early warning when the recognition system considers it necessary. In Fig. 8 is showed a typical EWBS working in conjunction with ISDB-T. At this stage, the system is able to recognize LP and VT microseisms. To provide practical alerts, incremental ranges of LP and VT events were defined and linked to existing emergency types: green (0 to 199 events), yellow (200 to 399 events), and red (400 or more events).

For the EWBS system, in order to monitor the signal from the air and replicate the message sent by the EWBS transmission, to do that, we use an ADALM-PLUTO, which is a low-cost, portable SDR platform developed by Analog Devices. It is designed to provide users with a flexible and affordable solution for learning and experimenting with wireless communication systems. The device combines the capabilities of a high-performance SDR with a user-friendly interface, making it accessible to both beginners and experienced users. The ADALM-PLUTO device is utilized as a receiver within the EWBS system. It serves the purpose of analyzing the physical and transport layers of the broadcast signal, decoding area codes, and the overlaid message. The system uses the capabilities of the ADALM-PLUTO receiver to capture and process the transmitted alerts, and then re-transmits them by an internal network to connected devices for further dissemination. This allows efficient and timely distribution of emergency alerts

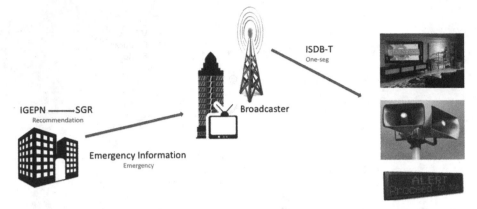

Fig. 8. EWBS system and ISDB-T integration.

to individuals and communities, in which the alert is then retransmitted by an internal network, which acts as a gateway and sends it to devices connected to the network. Finally, the response time of the EWBS system is evaluated when a change in alert is issued. Automatic recognition system for microseisms has an event counter. Each time it exceeds a certain number of events, which is related to an alert, for our practical case, a 1-h observation time was defined. For every 200 recognized events, the alert changes from green to yellow. Upon exceeding 400 events, the alert changes from yellow to red and the EWBS system is activated. The EWBS system introduces a t_p of 30-s delay in broadcasting overlay messages on television receivers with the message "Eruption threat, evacuation order for Sangolquí." Figure 9 shows a snap-shop of the complete system.

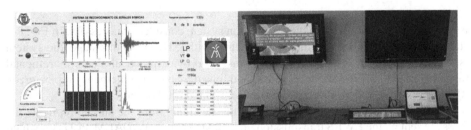

Fig. 9. EWBS system for the Cotopaxi volcano.

4 Conclusion and Future Work

This paper shows that it was possible to develop an automatic recognition system of microseisms of the Cotopaxi volcano, where supervised learning models k-NN, DT, and SVM were obtained and implemented in the LP, VT, TR, and HYB event detection systems, and LP and event classification. VT is based on characteristics in the frequency domain, where three detection models and three classification models were obtained; with these models, a voting system for detecting microseisms was carried out, achieving a BER of 0.01. In the case of the classifier, the system reaches a BER of 0.11.

The results showed a 7% increase in accuracy compared to the previous test, demonstrating improved performance. However, 11 earthquakes were still misclassified. Integration of these classifiers with a voting system improves their performance. The selected set of 50 features plays a crucial role in achieving accurate results. The recognition system and the activation of the EWBS system presents a t_p of 30-s delay, which is optimal for this type of application, which allows, in the event of an eventual eruption, to safeguard the lives and resources of the populations surrounding the Cotopaxi volcano.

As a future work, our research group is interested in continuing with the research together with the IGEPN and the SGR to define the possible ranges that allow alert changes and activate the EWBS system in a timely manner.

References

1. Gaetano, P., Calvello, M., Piciullo, L.: Monitoring strategies for local landslide early warning systems. Landslides **16**(2), 213–231 (2019)
2. Haritharaj, S., Visakh, N.U., Antony, A.C.: Early warning systems: an alert to flood. Vigyan Varta **1**(1), 30–32 (2020)
3. Rahayu, H., Comfort, L., Haigh, R., et al.: A study of people-centered early warning system in the face of near-field tsunami risk for Indonesian coastal cities. Int. J. Disaster Resil. Built Environ. **11**(2), 241–262 (2020)
4. LaBrecque, J., et al.: Global navigation satellite system enhancement for tsunami early warning systems. Global Assessment Report on Disaster Risk Reduction (2019)
5. Zhang, M., et al.: Brief communication: effective earthquake early warning systems: appropriate messaging and public awareness roles. Nat. Hazards Earth Syst. Sci. **21**(10), 3243–3250 (2021)
6. Adi, W., et al.: Earthquake early warning system using ncheck and hard-shared orthogonal multitarget regression on deep learning. IEEE Geosci. Remote Sens. Lett. **19**, 1–5 (2021)
7. Shin, A., et al.: MOWLAS: NIED observation network for earthquake, tsunami and volcano. Earth Planets Space **72**(1), 1–31 (2020)
8. Stovall, W., Wilkins, A., Mandeville, C., Driedger, C.: U.S. Geological Survey Volcano Hazards Program—Assess, forecast, prepare, engage. U.S. Geological Survey Fact Sheet. 2016–3040, 4p. (2016). https://doi.org/10.3133/fs20163040
9. Bjerge, B., et al.: Technology and information sharing in disaster relief. PLoS ONE **11**(9), e0161783 (2016)
10. Fearnley, C.J., et al.: Standardisation of the USGS volcano alert level system (VALS): analysis and ramifications. Bull. Volcanol. **74**, 2023–2036 (2012)
11. Macherera, M., Chimbari, M.J.: A review of studies on community based early warning systems. Jàmbá J. Disaster Risk Stud. **8**(1) (2016)
12. Sparks, R., Biggs, J., Neuberg, J.: Monitoring volcanoes. Science, 1310–1311 (2021)
13. Lowenstern, J., et al.: Guidelines for volcano-observatory operations during crises: recommendations from the 2019 volcano observatory best practices meeting. J. Appl. Volcanol. **11**(1), 1–24 (2022)
14. Pallister, J., et al.: Volcano observatory best practices workshops-a summary of findings and best-practice recommendations. J. Appl. Volcanol. **8**(1), 1–33 (2019)

15. Lara-Cueva, R., Benítez, D., Carrera, E., Ruíz, M., Rojo, J.: Automatic recognition of long period events from volcano tectonic earthquakes at cotopaxi volcano. IEEE Trans. Geosci. Remote Sens. **54**(9), 5247–5257 (2016)

16. Corominas, O., Martí, J.: Estudio comparativos de los planes de actuación frente al riesgo volcánico (Chile, Costa Rica, El Salvador, Ecuador, Espeña, México y Nicaragua), Revista Geológica de América Central (2011)

17. IGEPN: Volcanes más activos del Ecuador (2020). https://www.igepn.edu.ec/

18. Ortiz Herazo, H.: Estudio de los Efectos de Sitio para la Construcción de un Índice de Actividad Sísmica en el volcán Cotopaxi. Escuela Politécnica Nacional (2013)

19. IGEPN: Cotopaxi (2017). https://www.igepn.edu.ec

20. Lara, R., Benítez, D., Carrera, V., Ruiz, M., Rojo Álvarez, R.: Feature selection of seismic waveforms for long period event detection at Cotopaxi Volcan. J. Volcanol. Geotherm. Res. **316**, 34–49 (2016)

21. Pérez, N., et al.: ESeismic: towards an ecuadorian volcano seismic repository. J. Volcanol. Geotherm. Res. **396**, 106855 (2020)

Using Eye Tracking to Map Attention in an EEG-Based Brainwave Graphic Visualization System

Valdecir Becker[(⊠)] , Matheus Cavalcanti , Felipe Melo , Thiago Silva ,
and Matheus Falcão

Laboratory of Interaction and Media, Informatics Center, Federal University of Paraíba, João
Pessoa - PB, Brazil
valdecir@ci.ufpb.br

Abstract. This article describes the incorporation of eye tracking in a brainwaves
visualization and analysis system, based on electroencephalography (EEG). The
visualization system was developed in Python, using a Emotiv Insight headset,
to analyze the fruition of audiovisual content. During the tests, there was a need
to identify whether the reactions mapped by the EEG were in fact related to
the enjoyment of the content or whether they originated from external elements,
with the individual looking away from the screen and, consequently, losing his
attention. Based on the Design Science Re-search methodology, eye tracking was
incorporated into the system architecture. For validation, tests were performed
with 10 users, using a movie trailer. Analyzing the generated data, it was possible
to identify the correlation between the information presented by the EEG and the
gaze of the individuals. In this way, it is possible to increase certainty about the
origin of emotions during the fruition of audiovisual content.

Keywords: Eye Tracking · EEG · Audiovisual Fruition

1 Introduction

Eye tracking technology is well known and used in several areas of knowledge, such
as usability research, marketing, cognitive psychology experiments or as entertainment
and games. Its operation is based on detecting the movement of a user's eyes during
interaction. This can be done through different tools: webcams, infrared cameras, glasses,
head-mounted displays. The collected data can provide relevant information about users,
such as their attention to a certain object on the screen, for example.

This technology is flexible and can be used with other tools, such as brainwave readers
and viewers. In previous stages of this research, a brainwave visualization system based
on electroencephalography (EEG) was developed (9, 10). The objective was to map
emotions during the fruition process of audiovisual content mapping changes in neural
wave patterns. However, a problem that arose during the tests was related to the focus and
origins of emotions, which in some cases came from outside the TV screen. As a specific

M. J. Abásolo et al. (Eds.): jAUTI 2022, CCIS 1820, pp. 129–143, 2023.
https://doi.org/10.1007/978-3-031-45611-4_9

example, at a certain moment the cell phone of one of the participants rang, generating attention and a state of stress, identified by the measurement of brainwaves. However, for the purpose of the system, only emotions arising from audiovisual enjoyment are relevant.

In order to solve this problem, eye tracking was incorporated into the system via webcam, which allows identifying which elements of a scene the user is looking at or if his attention has been diverted to another subject outside the screen. For the tests, the user was shown a movie trailer while measuring their brainwaves through the EEG device Emotiv Insight and mapping the gaze directions. Thus, the objective of this article is to demonstrate how the use of eye tracking helped to identify the specific points on the screen that caught the user's attention, indicating what possibly caused the results observed through the visualization of the EEG waves.

The outcome demonstrates a clear correlation between the moments of attention generated by the film and the individual's gaze. By analyzing the attention identified reading brainwaves and comparing it with the gaze direction, it is possible to clearly infer which film elements, and where they were organized on the screen, aroused the viewer's curiosity. In this way, it is possible to have a greater degree of certainty that the attention, and consequently, the emotions felt by the individuals, were in fact generated by the film and not by external elements of the screen.

2 Eye Tracking

Interaction studies, as well as the entire Human Computer Interaction (HCI) field, is based on pointing, either to understand what is on screen, or to interact. In our everyday life, pointing is a natural way of approaching objects. Historically, the development of graphical user interfaces (GUIs) represents a significant advance in the usability of computers and their use by individuals. Pointing to an object that you can see is much easier than typing its name. Most GUI-based interactions, such as moving the cursor over text or selecting a fragment, choosing a menu item, clicking a hyperlink, or dragging an object, involve pointing. Usually, pointing operations are performed using specific hardware, such as a mouse, a trackball, a joystick, a track point, a touchpad, or a touch screen.

Another way of pointing to improve interaction is to capture images from the human eye, process them and perform an action. In other words, mapping the individual's gaze and, by identifying where he is looking, starting, or continuing the interaction. In this way, the appointment can be faster and more accurate, in addition to not involving specific hardware for data entry.

Eye tracking is a method that analyzes and identifies individual's visual attention (Fig. 1). With this technology, it is possible to determine the focus of attention, for how long and the progress in visual exploration. Eye tracking allows measurement of eye movements, eye positions and viewpoints through various technological processes. In other words, eye tracking identifies and monitors visual attention in terms of location, objects, and duration. Advanced image processing algorithms are then used to establish the gaze point related to the eye and stimuli [18, 27, 28].

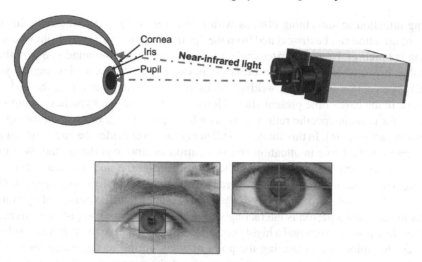

Fig. 1. A conceptual illustration of how eye-tracking technology works [18].

Eye movements represent an important feature of human movement, as they allow people to interact with others and with environments, analyzing, processing, and understanding the visual world. Computationally eye movements are assessed using eye tracking. This technique has been used in various professional fields including medical/health (particularly neurological conditions [19, 20]), psychology [21, 22], sports performance [23, 24], user experience and human-computer interaction [25, 26].

Over millennia, humans' eyes have evolved to process light, shape, color, focus and distance, making them sophisticated beings capable of performing complex tasks. In engineering terms, the eye and its muscles can be seen as a camera with image stabilization. Six muscles connect the eye to the head. The muscles are organized as antagonistic pairs and give the eye three degrees of freedom. One pair is responsible for horizontal movement, one pair controls vertical movement, and the third pair allows for rotational movement around the viewing direction. Together, the three pairs of muscles allow compensation for all head movements. To accomplish this task, the nerves that control the eye muscles are closely linked to the balance organ located in the ear [17].

Still in terms of engineering, the construction of the eye itself is similar to that of a camera. There is a diaphragm, called iris for the eye, which allows to adjust the aperture. The hole in the iris is called pupil. In contrast to a camera that uses a lens with a fixed focal length and achieves focus by changing its position, the eye's lens can change the focal length by changing the shape of the lens. The light sensitive area is the inner back surface of the eye and is named retina.

Theoretically, the main guideline for using eye movement analysis in UX and HCI research is named the "mind-eye hypothesis" [30, 31] or "attention-eye assumption" [32]. In this hypothesis there is a very close relationship between what the eyes are looking at and what the mind is focusing on. In other words, there is an intimate connection between the direction of gaze and the information that is in the focus of a person's attention. This is a very important assumption, as people can be clearly looking at something, but paying attention to something else, as with mind wandering [33], where the internal focus of attention can be dissociated from the "point of view" (i.e., away from where the person is looking). However, extensive evidence suggests that the mind-eye hypothesis probably holds when inputting information is done visually. Examples are: during a reading, perception in a scene, writing, interaction with computers or in the audience of films, in the case of the present study. However, the mind-eye hypothesis admits the demand for domain-specific refinements, as when applied to geometric reasoning and other abstractions [34]. In this study it is still necessary to consider the audio, which also plays an important role in attention and generation of emotions during the enjoyment of movies. Looking and listening are often combined in the audio-visual experience. Although relevant, audio was not considered in this study, which focuses on eye tracking.

In the HCI context, the mind-eye hypothesis implies that recordings of eye movements made when a person is interacting with a visual interface can provide a dynamic trace of their point of view and a highly correlated index of where their attention is being directed. Mapping and measuring the point of view during the interface interactions of individuals and making some inferences about the processing of attention fundamentally depends on the measurement of "eye fixations". These are moments when the eyes are relatively stationary, so that information can be captured and coded more accurately. Measuring fixations essentially reveals the amount of attentional processing being applied to objects or visual elements within the screen or interface [29].

In a simplified way, there are two types of eye trackers: Screen based eye trackers and Wearable eye trackers [27, 28]. The first type is completely non-intrusive, recording eye movement from a distance. It is normally integrated with the monitor and interferes less in the evaluation processes. The most common mechanical setup is a stationary eye tracker. These systems are commercially available as a laboratory tool and are typically used in medical or marketing research. In addition to the desktop computer with an integrated eye tracker, software is needed to analyze and visualize data from the users' gaze. Although medical eye trackers usually have a chin rest for head fixation, marketing research demands systems with additional head tracking, making movements more natural, free from any obstacles.

The second type gives freedom of movement to the user, as it is wearable (like glasses, for example). In this case, three cameras are used. One films the environment in front of the individual and two films the eyes. A software makes the triangulation between the filmed landscape and the gaze direction.

2.1 Video Based Eye Tracking

As described, video-based eye tracking estimates gaze direction by analyzing images taken by video cameras. The most used technique is iris detection based on the high contrast between the white of the eye and the dark of the iris. Studies have shown that this method has good horizontal accuracy and poor vertical accuracy. This happens because the upper and lower part of the iris is covered by the eyelid, reducing the field for mapping movements. There are two ways to detect pupil position and movement. The first, called the dark pupil method, locates the position of a black pupil in the image generated by the camera. This can be problematic for dark brown eyes, where the contrast between the brown iris and black pupil is very low. The second method, called bright pupil or pupil center-corneal reflection (PCCR), uses infra-red light reflected off the retina, inverting the contrast between the pupil and the rest of the eyeball. In this way, the pupil appears white in the camera image, an effect similar to "red eyes" in flash photographs. PCCR requires illumination with infrared light. That is, there is a need to incorporate the generation of this light in the eye tracking camera [17, 28].

In the literature, the combination of EEG with eye tracking tools to improve emotion recognition techniques can be observed in Lu et al., proving to be positive, with an accuracy of 87.59% using a fuzzy integral to perform data fusion [2]. In Lopez-Gil et al., we see another application to improve emotion recognition based on EEG, eye tracking and other biometric signals [3]. In the context of content recommendation systems, Xu et al. uses data referring to user attention to items on an online platform of documents, images, and videos, obtained through eye tracking, to recommend new content in a personalized way [4]. Eye tracking can also be seen in usability research [5] and in neuromarketing [6], as a tool to predict individual's usage/consumption pattern.

For a better understanding of how eye tracking technology works and how it can provide relevant data for analyzing user's interest, taste, or emotional state, it is important to understand more deeply some terms that will help define what types of information will be observed when carrying out an eye tracking experiment (Fig. 2).

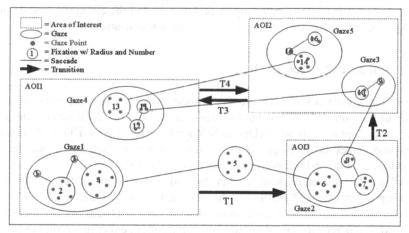

Fig. 2. Visual representation of terms related to understanding eye tracking [7].

The first term "gaze point", which refers to the specific points of the image user looked at. A set of gaze points grouped in a certain space in a certain period is named fixation [7]. This region is of paramount importance for our study, as it is during its occurrence that user's main cognitive processes occur, such as comprehension and memory.

The rapid movement performed between fixation areas is named a saccade. During its occurrence, which corresponds between 30 and 80 ms, the visual information is suppressed. A set of fixations can be grouped by proximity in a gaze, which in turn is organized into areas of interest (AOI) [7]. The time spent on each AOI (dwell time) can be a factor that will define user's interest in a given stimulus presented on the screen, and a longer time spent can mean a higher level of interest. One way to observe this

Fig. 3. Heat map obtained through eye tracking [8].

phenomenon, which was used in this work, is through heat maps, which will show on the screen the points that caught the user's attention [8], as shown in Fig. 3.

Using the information indicated above, associated with data obtained through the EEG, it is possible to generate a diagnosis regarding user's perception of visual stimuli. This allows for a better understanding of preferences and the emotional and cognitive processes that naturally occur as content on a screen is consumed.

3   Design Science Research

In this research, eye tracking software for a webcam was used, with the aim of helping to identify user's points of interest about scenes of a movie trailer displayed on the screen. Research development is based on Design Science Research (DSR). This methodological process legitimizes the development of problem-oriented artifacts as an important way to produce scientific and technological knowledge [11–13].

DSR was considered relevant for this study after identifying gaps in technical and scientific production in the field of audiovisual systems. For DSR, a fundamental element is understanding the external and internal environments about the artifact to be created. It was found that, in recent years, there has been no mention, either in the HCI or in media studies fields, about creation of models, methods or structures capable of supporting graphic visualizations of brainwaves, with gaze mapping, during the content fruition process of audiovisual systems [14].

By the structure of the DSR method, the process starts with a mental model of a possible solution (recalling that DSR does not look for ideal solutions, but possible artifacts that generate a viable result [14]). A mental model can be described as a small-scale reality, constructed from perception, imagination, or speech understanding. Mental models are similar to architects' models or physicists' diagrams, as their structure is analogous to the situation they represent [15]. A process model should provide some guidance, as reviewers, editors, and consumers, on what to expect from DSR survey results. March and Smith [16] contributed to this expectation with their thoughts on the research outcomes. Hevner et al. [13] enlarged this expectation by describing the essential elements of DSR research.

The stages of this method can be systematized into six activities:

Activity 1: Identification and motivation of problems. This step defines the specific research problem and justifies the value of a solution. As the problem definition will be used to develop an artifact that will effectively provide a solution, it can be useful to atomize the problem conceptually so that the solution can capture its complexity. Justifying the value of a solution has two impacts: it motivates the researcher and his audience to pursue the solution and accept the results; helps to understand the reasoning associated with the researcher's understanding of the problem. Resources needed for this activity include knowledge of the problem state and the importance of its solution.

Activity 2: Define the goals of a solution. This step aims at inferring the objectives of a solution from the definition of the problem and knowledge of what is possible and feasible. Objectives can be quantitative, such as terms in which a desirable solution would be better than the current ones, or qualitative, such as a description of how a new artifact is expected to support solutions to hitherto unaddressed problems. Objectives must be rationally inferred from the problem specification. Resources needed to do this include knowledge of the problem state and current solutions, if any, and their effectiveness.

Activity 3: Design and development. In this step the artifact is actually created. Such artifacts are potentially constructs, models, methods, or instantiations (each broadly defined) or novel properties of technical, social, and/or informational resources [10]. Conceptually, a design research artifact can be any designed object on which a research contribution is incorporated. This activity includes determining the artifact's desired functionality and architecture, and then creating the actual artifact. Resources needed to move from objectives to design and development include knowledge of theory that can be applied to a solution.

Activity 4: Demonstration. In this step the researcher must demonstrate the use of the artifact to solve one or more instances of the problem. This may involve its use in experimentation, simulation, case study, testing or other appropriate activity. Resources needed for the demo include effective knowledge of how to use the artifact to solve the problem.

Activity 5: Evaluation. Step where one observes and evaluates how well the artifact supports a solution to the problem. This activity involves comparing the goals of a solution to the actual results observed from using the artifact in the demo. It requires knowledge of relevant metrics and analysis techniques. Depending on the nature of the problem site and the artifact, the evaluation can take many forms. It may include items such as a comparison of artifact functionality to the solution goals from Activity 2, objective quantitative measures of performance such as budgets or items produced, results of satisfaction surveys, customer feedback, or simulations. It can include quantifiable measures of system performance, such as response time or availability. Conceptually, this assessment can include any appropriate empirical evidence or logical proof. At the end of this activity, researchers can decide whether to go back to Activity 3 to try to improve the effectiveness of the artifact or continue with the communication and leave further improvements to subsequent projects. The nature of the survey location may determine whether this iteration is feasible.

Activity 6. Communication. Finally, this step discloses the problem and its importance, the artifact, its usefulness and novelty, the rigor of its design and its effectiveness to researchers and other relevant audiences, such as professional routines, where appropriate. In academic research publications, researchers can use the structure of this process to organize the paper, as well as the nominal structure of an empirical research process (problem definition, literature review, hypothesis development, data collection, analysis, results, discussion, and conclusion), considering a common framework for empirical research papers. Communication requires knowledge of the disciplinary culture.

This article describes the use of the online tool GazeRecorder, an online software for eye tracking experiments based on computer cameras. For the demonstration and validation steps, an experiment was set up with a movie trailer. An initial calibration step was carried out with the user, which consists of following a red dot moving on the screen. Right after the calibration, the trailer was displayed on the screen for the user, who has his vision mapped. In this way, the tool is able to identify regions of the video where the user had the highest concentration. Finally, the software generates a heat map over the scenes, displaying the results of the experiment for further analysis. The software used has an accuracy of $1.05°$, a precision of $0.129°$ and a sampling frequency of 30 Hz [1].

4   Results and Discussion

To validate the artifact, an experiment was carried out involving 10 individuals, all male, mostly young and middle-aged people, members of the academic community of the Informatics Center of the Federal University of Paraíba. Users were exposed to the Black Phone movie's trailer, which has horror as its main feature.

During fruition, it is possible to notice that, when there were subtitles on the screen, users focused their vision on these textual elements (Fig. 4), presenting a quick transition from cinematographic elements to subtitles (saccades).

Fig. 4. Eye focus on the caption [Own authorship].

When there is not a single element in evidence, but several elements composing the scene, a greater dispersion of heat points in the eye tracking is noticeable (Fig. 5). This may indicate that the user may be looking for some crucial element of the scene or taking advantage of the moment to understand the environment in which the narrative takes place.

Fig. 5. Dispersion of the heat points [Own authorship].

Correlating with the EEG, in moments of jumpscare (unexpected jumps of something that can scare the viewer), the individuals had a high rate of Low Beta waves (a wave that can be interpreted as fear, tension, scares in a negative way). Comparing the eye tracking with these moments, it is possible to infer that the user was startled by the element that was in the scene, as there was a high ocular focus on this character in evidence (Fig. 6).

Fig. 6. Eye focus on a character in evidence [Own authorship].

Another correlation between the result of eye tracking and the EEG is in the scene shown in Fig. 7. At 29 s, we can notice the presence of an area of interest arranged over the central element of the scene. The character's figure appears in a dark and mysterious way, increasing the viewer's tension levels. This can be seen in the graph in Fig. 8, which shows a lot of Low Beta and High Beta wave activity at the same time. We can then deduce that the participant was anxious or afraid of the scene, focusing on the character and his actions.

Fig. 7. Eye Tracking in the scene at 29 s [Own authorship].

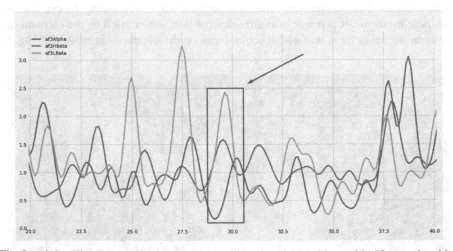

Fig. 8. Alpha, High Beta and Low Beta waves, with peak activity evident at 29 s [Own authorship].

It can be observed, by analyzing the graph, that around 80 and 85 s there is a decline in the alpha waves, while in eye tracking there is a constant focus on the character in the scene (Fig. 9). The suppression of these waves, identified in the electroencephalogram, can show significant correlations with a scene full of tension and suspense in the movie trailer (Fig. 10). When the participant is immersed in a moment of great focus and emotional involvement, it is common for alpha wave activity to decrease, indicating an increase in brain activation and cognitive concentration. During this intense scene, the reduction of alpha waves can denote an increase in the viewer's concentration and mental processing capacity, increasing the emotional connection and expectation in relation to the next events. This neurophysiological response can contribute to the suspense experience and intensify the emotional bond with the content presented in the movie trailer.

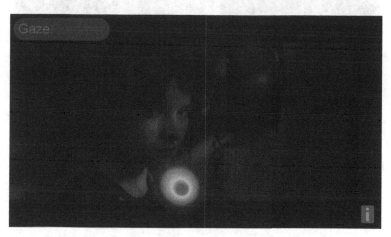

Fig. 9. Focus on the central character [Own authorship].

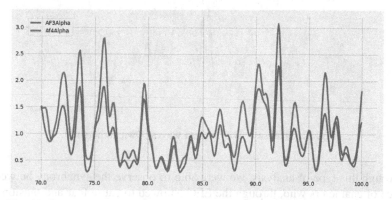

Fig. 10. Decline of alpha waves between seconds 80 and 85 [Own authorship].

The intense activity of beta waves, identified in the EEG (Fig. 12), may be associated with an energetic cognitive response and a state of heightened vigilance when the individual watches a trailer scene in which the antagonist is chasing the main character (Fig. 11). Beta waves, which occur in the frequency range of 12 to 30 Hz, have been linked to cognitive processing and the mobilization of mental resources. In this context, the high activity of beta waves may indicate an increase in the spectator's attention and vigilance in this scene full of action and danger. The intense pursuit involving the main character triggers an emotional response and generates greater neural activation, manifested by beta wave activity.

Fig. 11. Focus on the antagonist chasing the main character [Own authorship].

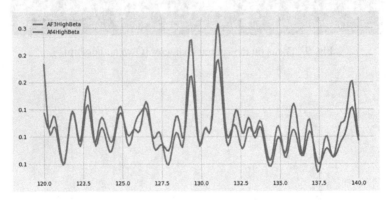

Fig. 12. Intense activity of beta waves [Own authorship].

Through this type of analysis, we were able to observe the synchrony between the presence of characters who, through the EEG, showed to cause fear and tension in the participants and the presence of fixations on their figure in the eye tracking. In this way, we confirm that the cause of the results verified in the EEG graphs were due to specific elements in the scene.

Therefore, the association between EEG and eye tracking allows us to infer information and characteristics about users that would not be detected using only one of the solutions. That is, the distinction between the scenographic elements that provoked reactions in the spectators is important for a future classification of users and scenes, based on their attributes.

5 Conclusions

This article demonstrated the use of eye tracking as an auxiliary tool in a research project using an EEG device to identify emotions. It is possible to state that the results of eye tracking were crucial in the analysis of brainwaves, as it allowed to associate the cinematographic elements that caught the user's attention, drawing a parallel of their brainwaves with the generated heatmap. It also made it possible to understand how the user responds to certain visual stimuli. In general, it is possible to state that eye tracking met the proposed objective and proved to be an excellent auxiliary tool.

As research limitations, we can emphasize the lack of a more comfortable environment for the user, and with less distractions, since the tests were carried out in a research laboratory, without emulating a cinema environment. Another limiting factor is the use of the notebook's webcam, which is considered inferior to other models available on the market, and which presented some small calibration problems. These calibration problems were suspected by times when the eye focus in the heatmap was a little more to the left or to the right of some element in evidence in the scene. In addition, the tests were performed with only 10 individuals, with similar characteristics in terms of age and training.

Therefore, as an improvement for future work, we can list a better camera for the tests, such as one that contains infrared. Another point of improvement is a more comfortable environment that provides less user distraction, so that there is no loss of information during the fruition process. In addition, it will be necessary to repeat the tests with a larger number of individuals, in order to identify neural reading patterns that allow for an in-depth analysis of the mapped emotions.

References

1. Simply, U.: User Experience Lab. The comparison of accuracy and precision of eye tracking: GazeFlow vs. SMI RED 250 (2013)
2. Lu, Y., et al.: Combining eye movements and EEG to enhance emotion recognition. In: Proceedings of the Twenty-Fourth International Joint Conference on Artificial Intelligence (IJCAI 2015), vol. 15, pp. 1170–1176 (2015)
3. López-Gil, J.M., et al.: Method for Improving EEG Based Emotion Recognition by Combining It with Synchronized Biometric and Eye Tracking Technologies in a Non-invasive and Low Cost Way. Front. Comput. Neurosci. **10**, 85 (2016)
4. Xu, S., et al.: Personalized online document, image and video recommendation via commodity eye-tracking. In: RecSys'08, pp. 83–90 (2008)
5. Alex, P., Ball, L.: Eye tracking in human-computer interaction and usability research: current status and future prospects (2010)
6. Santos, R.D., et al.: Eye tracking in neuromarketing: a research agenda for marketing studies. Int. J. Psychol. Stud. **7**(1), 32 (2015)
7. Blascheck, T., et al. State-of-the-art of visualization for eye tracking data. In: Eurographics Conference on Visualization (EuroVis), p. 29 (2014)
8. Farnsworth, B.: 10 Most Used Eye Tracking Metrics and Terms, iMotions (2020)
9. DA Silva, T., Tavares, C., Cavalcanti, M.D., Becker, V.: Desenvolvimento de um sistema para visualização gráfica de ondas neurais durante consumo de conteúdos midiáticos. IV Jornada Internacional GEMInIS (JIG 2021) (2021)

10. Becker, V., et al.: A system for graphical visualization of brainwaves to analyse media content consumption. In: International Conference on Human-Computer Interaction. Springer, Cham, pp. 318–328 (2022). https://doi.org/10.1007/978-3-031-05409-9_24
11. Dresch, A., Lacerda, D.P., Junior, J.A.: Design science research: método de pesquisa para avanço da ciência e tecnologia. Bookman Editora (2020)
12. Järvinen, P.: Action research is similar to design science. Qual. Quant. **41**(1), 37–54 (2007)
13. Hevner, A.R., March, S.T., Park, J.: Design research in information systems research. MIS Q. **28**(1), 75–105 (2004)
14. Toscano, R.M., de Souza, H.B.A.M., da Silva Filho, S.G., Noleto, J.D., Becker, V.: HCI methods and practices for audiovisual systems and their potential contribution to universal design for learning: a systematic literature review. In: Antona, M., Stephanidis, C. (eds.) HCII 2019. LNCS, vol. 11572, pp. 526–541. Springer, Cham (2019). https://doi.org/10.1007/978-3-030-23560-4_38
15. Johnson-Laird, P., Byrne, R.: A gentle introduction. Mental Models Website School Psychol. Trinity Coll. Dublin (2000)
16. March, S., Smith, G.: Design and natural science research on information technology. Decis. Support. Syst. **15**(4), 251–266 (1995)
17. Fitts, P.M.: The information capacity of the human motor system in controlling the amplitude of movement. J. Exp. Psychol. Gen. **121**(3), 262 (1992)
18. Bergstrom, J.R., Schall, A.: (eds.).: Eye Tracking in User Experience Design. Elsevier (2014)
19. Anderson, T.J., MacAskill, M.R.: Eye movements in patients with neurodegenerative disorders. Nat. Rev. Neurol. **9**, 74–85 (2013)
20. Molitor, R.J., Ko, P.C., Ally, B.A.: Eye movements in Alzheimer's disease. J. Alzheimers Dis. **44**, 1–12 (2015)
21. Hannula, D.E., et al.: Worth a glance: using eye movements to investigate the cognitive neuroscience of memory. Front. Hum. Neurosci. **4**, 166 (2010)
22. Armstrong, T., Olatunji, B.O.: Eye tracking of attention in the affective disorders: a meta-analytic review and synthesis. Clin. Psychol. Rev. **32**, 704–723 (2012)
23. Discombe, R.M., Cotterill, S.T.: Eye tracking in sport: a guide for new and aspiring researchers. Sport Exer. Psychol. Rev. **11**, 49–58 (2015)
24. Kredel, R., Vater, C., Klostermann, A., Hossner, E.-J.: Eye-tracking technology and the dynamics of natural gaze behavior in sports: a systematic review of 40 years of research. Front. Psychol. **8**, 1845 (2017)
25. Bergstrom, J.R., Schall, A.: Eye Tracking in User Experience Design. Elsevier (2014)
26. Goldberg, J.H., Wichansky, A.M.: Eye tracking in usability evaluation: a practitioner's guide. In: The Mind's eye. Elsevier, pp. 493–516 (2003)
27. Graham, L., Das, J., Moore, J., Godfrey, A., Stuart, S.: The eyes as a window to the brain and mind. In: Eye Tracking: Background, Methods, and Applications, pp. 1–14. New York, NY: Springer US (2022). https://doi.org/10.1007/978-1-0716-2391-6_1
28. Kasprowski, P.: Eye tracking hardware: past to present, and beyond. In: Stuart, S., (ed.) Eye Tracking: Background, Methods, and Applications, pp. 165–183. New York, NY: Springer US (2022). https://doi.org/10.1007/978-1-0716-2391-6_3
29. Ball, L.J., Richardson, B.H.: Eye movement in user experience and human–computer interaction research. In: Stuart, S., (ed.) Eye Tracking: Background, Methods, and Applications (pp. 165–183). Springer, New York (2022). https://doi.org/10.1007/978-1-0716-2391-6_10
30. Just, M.A., Carpenter, P.A.: Eye fixations and cognitive processes. Cogn. Psychol. **8**(4), 441–480 (1976)
31. Just, M.A., Carpenter, P.A.: A theory of reading: from eye fixations to comprehension. Psychol. Rev. **87**(4), 329 (1980)
32. Underwood, G., Everatt, J.: The role of eye movements in reading: some limitations of the eye-mind assumption. Adv. Psychol. **88**, 111–169. North-Holland (1992)

33. Smallwood, J., Schooler, J.W.: The science of mind wandering: empirically navigating the stream of consciousness. Annu. Rev. Psychol. **66**, 487–518 (2015)
34. Schindler, M., Lilienthal, A.J.: Domain-specific interpretation of eye tracking data: towards a refined use of the eye-mind hypothesis for the field of geometry. Educ. Stud. Math. **101**, 123–139 (2019)

Evaluating Perceived Value and Intention to Continue Using Over-the-Top Services in Latin America: A Case Study in Quito, Ecuador

Carina Haro Granizo[1]([✉]) [iD] and Gonzalo Olmedo[2] [iD]

[1] Universidad de las Fuerzas Armadas ESPE, Sangolquí, Ecuador
caharo4@espe.edu.ec
[2] WiCOM-Energy Research Group, Department of Electrical, Electronics, and Telecommunications, Universidad de las Fuerzas Armadas ESPE, Sangolquí, Ecuador
gfolmedo@espe.edu.ec

Abstract. The emergence of over-the-top (OTT) platforms in the early 21st century has revolutionized the distribution of multimedia content, replacing traditional physical methods with digital streaming services. As the popularity of OTT platforms continues to grow, the demand for these services has increased significantly worldwide. This article presents an investigation conducted in Quito, Ecuador, aimed at analyzing the value and technological acceptance of digital content services, with a focus on identifying the factors that contribute to the continuous usage of these platforms. A statistical data analysis methodology is employed to evaluate the influence of variables such as enjoyment, content, technological usability, cost, and security risk on the perceived value of the services. A structural equation model is proposed to analyze the hypotheses and examine the relationships between the variables. Additionally, the study identifies the most widely used OTT platforms that have gained significant acceptance among the population segments. The sample comprised 300 participants, and the data was processed, and hypotheses were tested using the PLS-SEM method. The findings of the analysis reveal a positive and significant relationship between the perception of value and the intention to use the platforms. Factors such as enjoyment, content quality, perceived fees, and security risks play a crucial role in shaping the perceived value and usage intention of the OTT platforms.

Keywords: Over-the-Top Platforms · Technological Acceptance · Perceived Value · Structural Equation Modeling · SmartPLS

1 Introduction

Digital media platforms, known as over-the-top (OTT), have witnessed substantial global growth attributed to the diverse content offerings and high-quality experiences facilitated by new Internet infrastructures [1, 2]. Prominent OTT applications like Netflix,

---

The original version of the chapter has been revised. A correction to this chapter can be found at https://doi.org/10.1007/978-3-031-45611-4_11

© The Author(s), under exclusive license to Springer Nature Switzerland AG 2023, corrected publication 2023
M. J. Abásolo et al. (Eds.): jAUTI 2022, CCIS 1820, pp. 144–160, 2023.
https://doi.org/10.1007/978-3-031-45611-4_10

Disney Plus, Amazon Prime, and Apple TV+ have become common household names, offering audio and video content through subscription-based services, thereby capturing a significant share of the global market. The transition from cable or satellite television to OTT applications has fueled intense competition to acquire and retain customers [3], leading to a highly competitive landscape within the OTT industry.

According to [4], OTT platforms are projected to experience a remarkable annual growth rate of 29% between 2021 and 2028 worldwide. In Latin America, the percentage of households with OTT subscriptions stood at 26% in 2021, with estimates suggesting a rise to 35% by 2026 [5].

Over the past years, an increasing number of studies have delved into the examination of customer satisfaction levels and the determinants that influence users' decisions to continue using OTT platforms. These investigations have been conducted in diverse countries, including India [6] and Korea [7], showcasing the global relevance of understanding users' preferences and behaviors in the digital media landscape.

Notably, the emergence of the COVID-19 pandemic has significantly impacted media consumption patterns worldwide [8]. The study in question sheds light on this aspect, particularly highlighting the notable shift towards OTT content consumption during the pandemic. The utilization of the PLS-SEM model to explore the influence of customer engagement and service experience quality on users' inclination to continue using streaming services adds rigor to the analysis, providing a comprehensive understanding of the underlying relationships. Moreover, the research emphasizes the utmost significance of focusing on customer engagement and user experience as pivotal factors influencing future subscription decisions. By recognizing the importance of creating an emotionally engaged customer base, service providers can nurture stronger relationships with their users, leading to higher retention rates and increased brand loyalty. Additionally, the suggestion to offer personalized packages showcases the need for customization and tailoring content offerings to cater to individual user preferences, a strategy that resonates well with contemporary consumers seeking personalized experiences. The study also addresses the option of advertising-supported content, presenting an alternative approach to subscription-based models. Understanding the potential trade-offs between these two approaches is crucial for service providers in aligning their business strategies with users' preferences and demands.

In [9], a framework is presented for evaluating the Quality of Experience (QoE) of a service, encompassing both functional and non-functional requirements. Non-functional requirements are classified into objective, subjective, and business parameters that impact the Quality of Service (QoS), Quality of Experience (QoE), and Quality of Business (QoBiz), respectively. Given the strong interdependence among these metrics, the study explores how to assess the QoE of a web-based OTT service, taking into account subjective, objective, and business parameters. The functional behavior of the service is described using an Extended Finite State Machine (EFSM) that tracks the non-functional objective, subjective, and business-related parameters through context variables and corresponding updating functions. These parameters are used to evaluate the service's QoE. The study demonstrates that the corresponding model allows for monitoring the interaction between the user and the service, integrating subjective, objective, and business parameters, thereby making it applicable for QoE evaluation in any OTT service.

The present study aims to replicate the evaluation model of perceived value and intention to continue using Over-The-Top (OTT) services within Latin America, with a specific focus on the city of Quito in Ecuador. The research methodology involves designing a survey based on validated constructs and questions from existing literature. Structural Equation Models (SEMs) will be utilized to analyze and assess the results obtained from the survey. Through this investigation, valuable insights will be gained regarding the perceived value of OTT services and users' intention to continue using them in the context of Quito, Ecuador.

2 Model Research and Hypotheses Development

The present study employed the research model introduced in [7] to examine OTT user satisfaction and their intention to continue using the service within the population of Quito. The model is based on the Value-Based Adoption Model (VAM), which identifies utility, enjoyment, technological features, and perceived cost as the key determinants of perceived value and intention to use [10].

Figure 1 provides a visual representation of the proposed model, which incorporates six exogenous variables serving as antecedents to the positive factors (content, enjoyment, and usability) and negative factors (technology, perceived fee, and security risk). These factors, in turn, exert an influence on the endogenous variables of perceived value in relation to usage satisfaction and intention to continue using the service. The exogenous variables represent latent constructs, while the observable variables are derived from survey results, providing empirical support for the model's framework. Through this comprehensive approach, the study aims to gain a deeper understanding of the complex dynamics influencing users' perceptions and behaviors in the realm of OTT services.

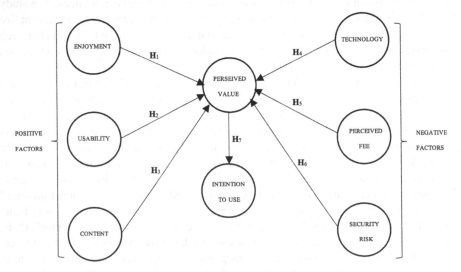

Fig. 1. OTT platform Research Model.

Based on the aforementioned, it is deemed interesting to propose the following hypotheses to investigate the relationship between positive and negative factors on perceived value and intention to use OTT systems in the city of Quito.

H_1: Entertainment has a direct and positive impact on perceived value.

H_2: Usability has a direct and positive impact on perceived value.

H_3: Content has a direct and positive impact on perceived value.

H_4: Technology has a direct and positive impact on perceived value.

H_5: Perceived cost has a direct and positive impact on perceived value.

H_6: Security risk has a direct and positive impact on perceived value.

H_7: Perceived value has a direct and positive impact on the intention to continue using the OTT platform.

These hypotheses will be tested through the analysis of data collected from surveys and evaluated using appropriate statistical methods to examine the relationships between the factors and variables under investigation.

3 Methodology

The hypotheses regarding perceived value and intention to use will be evaluated using a quantitative scientific methodology, employing an online survey supported by a comprehensive structural model.

To validate the measurement scale and test the hypotheses proposed in the model, a variance-based structural equation analysis has been conducted [11]. The data processing and hypothesis testing have been performed using the PLS-SEM method through the SmartPLS software [12].

PLS-SEM is a multivariate analysis method primarily aimed at predicting dependent variables through robust model estimation. This program enables the analysis and determination of measurement and structural model estimation considering the dependent variables. It also allows for the calculation and quantification of the size of both indirect and direct effects that certain variables in this model have on others [13]. This method has the advantage of not imposing the direction of the hypotheses, making it the most reliable and recommended approach [14].

The composition of the proposed model, which includes reflective and formative variables, makes this technique and software optimal for the analysis proposed in the study [15].

3.1 Online Survey Design

The percentage of households in Ecuador utilizing OTT services in 2020 was reported to be 21% [5]. Furthermore, projections suggest that the average number of households with OTT services in Latin America is expected to reach 28% by 2022 [5]. In our study, we focused specifically on the Quito canton, utilizing the latest available census data from 2010, which indicated a total population of 2,239,191 inhabitants [16]. Assuming an average of 4 members per household, the estimated total number of households in the Quito canton amounts to 559,798.

To determine the required sample size for our study, we applied Cochran's formula for a finite population [17]. This formula considers factors such as the desired level of confidence and the acceptable margin of error. By considering a confidence level of 95% and a margin of error of 5%, we calculated that a sample size using the following expression:

$$n = \frac{p(1-p)}{\frac{e^2}{z^2} + \frac{p(1-p)}{N}},$$ (1)

where:

n = sample size
N = population size (559,798 households).
e = acceptable sampling error (5%).
p = the population proportions (21% of households had the OTT service by 2020).
z = z value at reliability level 95% or significance level 0.05 ($z = 1.96$).

Based on this formula, a minimum sample size of $n = 255$ surveys were determined.

A survey instrument was developed for data collection, incorporating the constructs and questions proposed in the relevant literature [7]. The Likert scale was employed as the measurement scale for all the questions, allowing respondents to indicate their level of agreement or disagreement [18]. The use of the Likert scale in the survey instrument allowed for the collection of quantitative data, facilitating statistical analysis, and providing valuable insights into the perceptions and opinions of the respondents. This approach enhances the robustness and reliability of the research findings.

The survey was administered to a total of 300 participants in the Quito canton. The respondents were predominantly within the age range of 20 to 55 years, as illustrated in Fig. 2. The sample composition reflects a diverse representation of the population, contributing to the generalizability of the study findings.

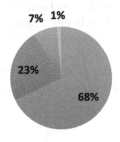

■ From 20-35 years ■ From 36-45 years

■ From 46-55 years ■ Over 55 years

Fig. 2. Age of the population that was interviewed - 300 samples in Quito.

To ensure the validity and reliability of the survey instrument, a confirmatory factor analysis was conducted. This rigorous analysis helped identify the most significant items for each construct, which are presented in Table 1, providing valuable insights for the study.

Table 1. Constructs, codes and items for the questionnaire.

Construct	Code	Items
Enjoyment	EN1	Frequency at which the content of OTT platforms helps to relax and provides entertainment during leisure time
	EN2	Perception of the positive impact of using OTT platforms on quality of life
Usability	US1	Ease of selecting and managing content on OTT platforms
	US2	Familiarity with how to view or change personal information on OTT platforms
	US3	Knowledge of the number of devices that can be used simultaneously on OTT platforms with the account
Content	CONT1	Satisfaction in finding all desired content in the preferred language on the utilized OTT platform
	CONT2	Perceived usefulness of the ratings or ratings displayed for each content on an OTT platform
Technology	TEC1	Importance given to the use of more sophisticated technologies in the utilized OTT services
	TEC2	Importance of the OTT service supporting multiple devices
Perceive Fee	PF1	Rating of the cost of the currently used OTT service compared to the available content
	PF2	Willingness to acquire additional peripherals to enhance the viewing experience on the utilized OTT platform
Security Risk	SE1	Familiarity with security measures to prevent unauthorized access to the account on OTT platforms
	SE2	Feeling of security when entering credit card information on OTT platforms
Perceived Value	PV1	Frequency of sharing information about series, movies, documentaries, or other consumed content with family and friends
	PV2	Frequency of using OTT systems for entertainment
	PV3	Level of satisfaction with the currently used OTT service(s)
Intention to Use	IU1	Opinion on the automatic recommendations provided by the OTT platform based on previous choices
	IU2	Influence of recommendations from family or close acquaintances on the intention to use OTT platforms
	IU3	Plans to subscribe to new OTT platforms in the near future
	IU4	Probability of continuing to use OTT platforms in the next two years

After carefully identifying the main items for each construct, the questions utilized in the surveys were thoughtfully formulated to effectively capture participants' experiences with OTT platform services, as comprehensively presented in Table 2. This meticulous approach ensures the data collected is relevant and aligned with the research objectives.

Table 2. Constructs, codes and questions for the questionnaire.

Construct	Code	Questions
Enjoyment	EN1	How would you rate the entertainment offered by the current OTT service you are using?
	EN2	How often does watching content on OTT platforms help you relax and provide entertainment during your free time?
Usability	US1	How easy do you find it to select and navigate content on OTT platforms?
	US2	Are you familiar with how to view or change your personal information on OTT platforms?
	US3	Are you informed about the number of devices you can use simultaneously on OTT platforms with your account?
Content	CONT1	Do you find all the content you want to watch available in your preferred language on the OTT platform you use?
	CONT2	Would you be interested in having access to a free preview of some content before subscribing to an OTT platform?
Technology	TEC1	How important is the use of more sophisticated technologies in the OTT services you use?
	TEC2	How important is it for you that the current OTT service you use supports multiple devices?
Perceive Fee	PF1	Is the cost of the service an important factor in your decision to subscribe to an OTT platform?
	PF2	How would you rate the cost of the current OTT service you use compared to the available content?
Security Risk	SE1	Do you believe there is a risk of your personal information being compromised when uploading it to OTT platforms?
	SE2	Are you familiar with the security measures to prevent unauthorized access to your account on OTT platforms?
Perceived Value	PV1	How often do you share information about series, movies, documentaries, or other content you consume with your family and friends?
	PV2	How often do you use OTT systems for entertainment?
	PV3	How satisfied are you with the OTT service(s) you currently use?
Intention to Use	IU1	What is your opinion on the platform's automatic recommendations based on your previous choices?
	IU2	Have recommendations from family or close friends influenced your intention to use OTT platforms?
	IU3	Do you plan to subscribe to new OTT platforms in the near future?
	IU4	How likely are you to continue using OTT platforms over the next two years?

4   Analysis of the Results

Considering all the hypotheses and the coded items, the research model depicted in Fig. 3 is proposed.

To carry out the analysis of the proposed model, a measurement scale validation analysis must be conducted. Different criteria are applied to reflective and formative items during the validation of the measurement scale. For reflective items, individual reliability analysis, composite reliability, convergent validity, and discriminant validity are performed. These analyses can be found in Tables 3 and 4, respectively. Regarding formative variables, the collinearity of the indicators is assessed through the analysis of Variance Inflation Factor (VIF) and its weights [19].

First, the analysis proceeds with the individual reliability analysis of the study. The item loadings are examined. According to [20], these loadings should exceed 0.7. In this study, as presented in Table 3, all elements of the proposed first-order model surpass this cutoff threshold.

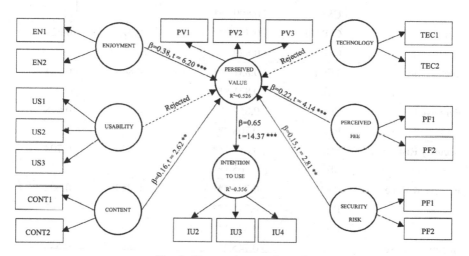

Fig. 3. Proposed research mode.

In this study, the validation analysis of the composite reliability scale is conducted, considering the Composite Reliability, which is a measure of internal reliability that evaluates how well different measures of a construct are correlated with each other and provide consistent and reliable measurements of the underlying concept. A value close to 1 indicates high internal reliability [21]. As observed in Table 3, all elements exceed the value of 0.7.

To assess the validity of each construct, the Average Variance Extracted (AVE) is utilized. AVE serves as a measure employed in confirmatory factor analysis within the structural equation model to evaluate convergent validity. Convergent validity pertains to the extent to which different measures of a construct exhibit correlation and accurately capture the intended concept. AVE is computed as the average of the shared variances among the construct's measures and their measurement errors. By comparing the calculated AVE against a threshold of 0.5, the adequacy of the construct's convergent validity is determined [22]. A value exceeding 0.5 indicates acceptable convergent validity, indicating that the proposed indicators account for at least 50% of the underlying variable's variance. In the present analysis, all items within the study surpass the cutoff threshold of 0.5, as presented in Table 3.

Table 3. Measurement items first order.

Construct	Code	Loading Factor	CR	AVE
Enjoyment	EN1	0.869 ***	0.847	0.735
	EN2	0.846 ***		
Usability	US1	0.775 ***	0.811	0.589
	US2	0.716 ***		
	US3	0.809 ***		
Content	CONT1	0.763 ***	0.771	0.627
	CONT2	0.820 ***		
Technology	TEC1	0.831 ***	0.840	0.724
	TEC2	0.871 ***		
Perceive Fee	PF1	0.857 ***	0.762	0.618
	PF2	0.708 ***		
Security Risk	SE1	0.813 ***	0.826	0.704
	SE2	0.865 ***		
Perceived Value	PV1	0.705 ***	0.819	0.602
	PV2	0.775 ***		
	PV3	0.842 ***		
Intention to Use	IU1	0.745 ***	0.829	0.549
	IU2	0.723 ***		
	IU3	0.731 ***		
	IU4	0.762 ***		

CR, Composite reliability; AVE, Average Variance Extracted.
$***p < 0.001$.

The validation of the measurement scale for the first-order variables involves conducting a discriminant validity analysis. For this case, Heterotrait-Monotrait analysis (HTMT) is employed, which is considered the most robust criterion in current literature [23]. This criterion considers that the variance captured by a variable from its indicators should be greater than the variance it shares with other variables [24]. Specifically, the values in the study should be less than 0.90 [25]. Here too, conducting the analysis in the proposed model, the item IU1 was eliminated as it did not meet the established criteria.

The HTMT values can be observed in Table 4, where the relationship between perceived value and perceived cost is at its limit.

Table 4. Measurement of the fist-order model - discriminant validity.

	Content	Enjoyment	Intention to Use	Perceive Fee	Perceived Value	Security Risk	Technicality	Usefulness
Content								
Enjoyment	0.583							
Intention to Use	0.866	0.601						
Perceive Fee	0.788	0.672	0.888					
Perceived Value	0.841	0.865	0.841	0.900				
Security Risk	0.646	0.363	0.551	0.881	0.680			
Technology	0.811	0.517	0.598	0.783	0.629	0.377		
Usability	0.791	0.433	0.569	0.694	0.614	0.606	0.761	

To conduct the structural analysis of the proposed model, it is essential to examine the presence of multicollinearity between the antecedent and endogenous variables. This is accomplished by assessing the structural variance inflation factor (VIF), whereby the structural model should exhibit values below 3, as recommended by [14]. In this study, the structural model adheres to this criterion, indicating the absence of structural multicollinearity, as all values are below 2, as shown in Table 5.

Table 5. Multicollinearity analysis.

	variance inflation factor (VIF)
Enjoyment → Perceived Value	1.226 ***
Content → Perceived Value	1.368 ***
Perceived Fee → Perceived Value	1.445 ***
Security Risk → Perceived Value	1.331 ***
Perceived Value → Intention to use	1.000 ***
Technology → Perceived Value	1.526 ***
Usability → Perceived Value	1.543 ***

*** $p < 0.001$

After conducting the analyses, a bootstrapping analysis with 50,000 samples is applied to assess the algebraic sign, magnitude, and significance of the proposed hypotheses. The algebraic sign analysis reveals that all hypotheses align with the expected direction. The Student's t-test and significance analysis indicate that hypotheses 1, 3, 5, 6, and 7 satisfy the criteria for both tests, whereas hypotheses 2 and 4 do not meet the criteria. Therefore, hypotheses H_2 (Usability → Perceived Value), and H_4 (Technology → Perceived Value) are rejected, while H_1 (Enjoyment → Perceived Value), H_3 (Content → Perceived Value), H_5 (Perceived fee → Perceived Value), H_6 (Security Risk → Perceived Value), and H_7 (Perceived Value → Intention to Use) are accepted (Fig. 4 and Table 6).

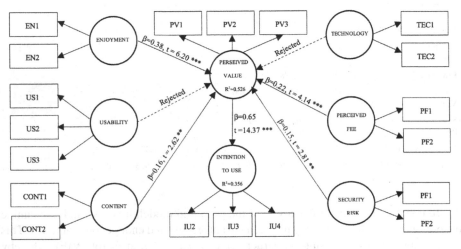

Fig. 4. Final Model.

Following the acceptance and rejection of hypotheses, the analysis of explained variance (R^2) and effect size (f^2) are conducted to assess the predictive relevance of the model [26]. The coefficient of determination R^2 represents the proportion of variance in an endogenous variable that is explained by the exogenous variables in the model, indicating the goodness of fit and predictive power of the exogenous variables on the endogenous variable. R^2 values around 0.25 or higher indicate a moderate to strong explanatory power of the exogenous variables on the endogenous variable. The R^2 values for Perceived Value (0.526) and Intention to Use (0.356) demonstrate a positive influence.

In addition, f^2 measures the contribution of an exogenous variable in explaining another endogenous variable. f^2 values around 0.02 are considered small, indicating a weak effect. f^2 values around 0.15 are considered medium, representing a moderate effect. f^2 values around 0.35 or higher are considered large, indicating a strong effect [27].

Table 6. Comparison of hypotheses.

Hypothesis		Path coefficient (β)	Statistics T	f^2
H_1	Enjoyment → Perceived Value	0.38 ***	6.18	0.241
H_3	Content → Perceived Value	0.16 **	2.63	0.039
H_5	Perceived Fee → Perceived Value	0.22 ***	4.14	0,071
H_6	Security Risk → Perceived Value	0.15 **	2.81	0,036
H_7	Perceived Value → Intention to use	0.65 ***	17.25	0,552

** $p < 0.01$, *** $p < 0.001$

IU R^2. 0.356; IU R^2 tight 0.354.

PV R^2 0.526; PV R^2 tight 0.516.

According to the others results, the most used OTT applications in Quito were registered, where Netflix is positioned in first place with 85.9%, and others applications like Disney +, HBO Max, STAR and Amazon Prime Video, it shows the Fig. 5.

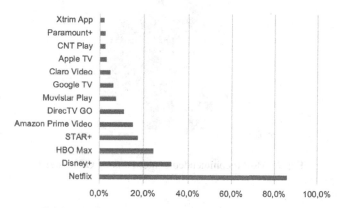

Fig. 5. Percentage of users for OTT platforms in Quito.

The survey also showed that TV is the most used device to view OTT content, with 52% based on the results presented in Fig. 6a, and that people prefer to watch high-resolution content, 4K, or HD, as shown by the results in Fig. 6b.

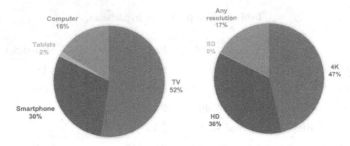

a. Most used OTT devices.   **b.** Preferred resolution quality.

Fig. 6. Devices and preferred quality to watch OTT content.

Regarding content's OTT preference, the most recommended among users were series, followed by movies and news or documentaries, as shown in Fig. 7.

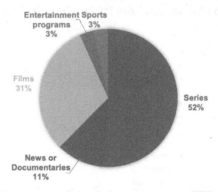

Fig. 7. Most recommended content among OTT users.

5   Discussion

The purpose of this study was to evaluate the perceived value and technological acceptance of digital content services, with a specific focus on over-the-top (OTT) platforms in Quito, Ecuador. The findings of the study demonstrated a positive and significant relationship between the perception of value and the intention to use these platforms. This aligns with previous research conducted on OTT platforms in various regions and underscores the influential role of perceived value in shaping user behavior.

To assess the hypotheses related to perceived value and intention to use, a quantitative scientific methodology was employed, utilizing an online survey supported by a comprehensive structural model. The data processing and hypothesis testing were conducted using the PLS-SEM method facilitated by the SmartPLS software. Given the composition of the proposed model, which involved both reflective and formative variables, this technique and software were deemed optimal for the analysis conducted in the study.

As part of the analysis, a bootstrapping analysis with 50,000 samples was performed to evaluate the algebraic sign, magnitude, and significance of the hypotheses. The results of the algebraic sign analysis indicated that all hypotheses were aligned with the expected direction. Subsequently, the Student's t-test and significance analysis were conducted to further scrutinize the hypotheses.

The rejection of hypotheses H_2 (Usability $\rightarrow$ Perceived Value) and H_4 (Technology $\rightarrow$ Perceived Value) suggests that usability and technology do not exert a direct impact on the perceived value of the digital content services examined in this study. Conversely, the acceptance of hypotheses H_1 (Enjoyment $\rightarrow$ Perceived Value), H3 (Content $\rightarrow$ Perceived Value), H_5 (Perceived fee $\rightarrow$ Perceived Value), H_6 (Security Risk $\rightarrow$ Perceived Value), and H_7 (Perceived Value $\rightarrow$ Intention to Use) emphasizes the significance of enjoyment, content quality, perceived fees, security risks, and perceived value in influencing user perceptions and intentions to use these platforms.

These findings hold notable implications for competitive practitioners and OTT service providers. By focusing on enhancing factors such as enjoyment, content quality, perceived fees, security measures, and perceived value, providers can better meet user preferences and expectations, ultimately leading to heightened user satisfaction and loyalty. Furthermore, understanding which factors, like usability and technology in this case, do not significantly influence perceived value enables providers to allocate their resources and efforts more effectively.

Moreover, comparing these findings with previous research conducted in different regions or countries would provide a broader perspective on the topic. Such comparative analysis can uncover similarities and differences in the factors influencing perceived value and intention to use OTT platforms, thereby shedding light on potential cross-cultural variations in user preferences and behaviors.

In summary, the acceptance of hypotheses H_1, H_3, H_5, H_6, and H_7 provides evidence of their significant relationship with perceived value. These findings contribute to the existing body of knowledge and offer valuable insights for OTT service providers to enhance user experiences and foster user engagement. The study's sample consisted of 300 participants, and the data processing and hypothesis testing were conducted using the PLS-SEM method. The analysis demonstrated a positive and significant relationship between the perception of value and the intention to use OTT platforms, with factors such as enjoyment, content quality, perceived fees, and security risks playing crucial roles in shaping the perceived value and usage intention of these platforms.

6 Conclusions

In this article, an analysis of the value perceived by the user of OTT platforms in the city of Quito and the intention to continue with the service was carried out. The study began with building a survey based on latent structures related to constructs with questions already validated in the literature in a structured model for research. Thus, six exogenous latent variables structured by the Value-Based Adoption (VAM) model were analyzed, which classifies positive factors (enjoyment, content and usability) and negative factors (technology, perceive fee and personal security risk) as the main factors of perceived value and analyzes intention of use. A structural equations model is proposed that is processed in SmartPLS. This model was successfully validated in terms of fit parameters.

There is a positive and significant relationship between perceived value and the intention to use OTT platforms. This finding supports previous research conducted in other regions and emphasizes the importance of perceived value in influencing user behavior.

Several key factors influence the perceived value of OTT platforms, including enjoyment, content quality, technological usability, perceived fees, and security risks. These factors play a crucial role in shaping user perceptions and their intention to use these platforms.

Usability and technology do not have a direct impact on the perceived value of the digital content services examined in this study. Therefore, OTT service providers should focus their efforts on enhancing other factors such as enjoyment, content quality, perceived fees, security measures, and perceived value to meet user preferences and expectations.

The findings have significant implications for competitive practitioners and OTT service providers. By improving the identified factors, providers can better cater to user preferences, leading to increased satisfaction and loyalty. Additionally, comparing these findings with previous research conducted in different regions or countries provides a broader perspective on the topic, highlighting potential cross-cultural variations in user preferences and behaviors.

In summary, this study highlights the importance of perceived value in the adoption and use of OTT platforms, while identifying key factors that influence perceived value. These conclusions offer practical guidance for OTT service providers and contribute to the existing body of knowledge in the field of technology and user behavior.

Additionally, results were shown where the most used OTT applications in the city of Quito are presented, as well as the preference of the technological equipment and resolution that users have the highest preference for, as well as the contents that have the highest recommendation among users.

Future researches could focus on this results to compare the situation on similar countries, and understand the best techniques to improve this services.

References

1. Chang, P.-C., Chang, H.-Y.: Exploring the factors influencing continuance usage of over-the-top services: the interactivity, consumption value, and satisfaction perspectives. Int. J. Technol. Hum. Interact. 16(4), 118–138 (2020). https://doi.org/10.4018/IJTHI.2020100108
2. Sudhir, A., Rao, P.: How technology is shaping the future of streaming services in India. Financ. Express (2021). https://www.financialexpress.com/brandwagon/how-technology-is-shaping-the-future-of-streaming-services-in-india/2162729
3. Fuduric, M., Malthouse, E.C., Lee, M.H.: Understanding the drivers of cable TV cord shaving with big data. J. Media Bus. Stud. 17(2), 172–189 (2020). https://doi.org/ https://doi.org/10.1080/16522354.2019.1701363
4. PWC. Global entertainment & media outlook 2021–2025. [Industry Growth Projections]. PricewaterhouseCoopers LLP 12. Outlook (2021). https://www.pwc.com/gx/en/entertainment-media/outlook-2021/perspectives-2021-2025.pdf
5. Jung, J., Melguizo A.: Is your netflix a substitute for your telefunken? evidence on the dynamics of tradition-al pay TV and OTT in Latin America. Telecommun. Policy. 47(1), 102397 (2022). ISSN 0308–5961

6. Chakraborty, D., Siddiqui, M., Siddiqui, A., Paul, J., Dash, G., Dal Mas, F.: Watching is valuable: consumer views – content consumption on OTT platforms. J. Retail. Cons. Serv. **70**, 103148 (2023). ISSN 0969–6989

7. Yoon, S.Y., Kim, J.B.: A study on user satisfaction and intention to continue use of OTT platform digital content provision service. In: 2022 IEEE/ACIS 7th International Conference on Big Data, Cloud Computing, and Data Science (BCD), pp. 290–296 (2022). https://doi.org/10.1109/BCD54882.2022.9900797

8. Gupta, G., Singharia, K.: Consumption of OTT media streaming in COVID-19 lockdown: insights from PLS analysis. Vision **25**(1), 36–46 (2021). https://doi.org/10.1177/097226292 1989118

9. Rivera, D., Kushik, N., Fuenzalida, C., Cavalli, A., Yevtushenko, N.: QoE Evaluation based on QoS and QoBiz parameters applied to an OTT Service. In: 2015 IEEE International Conference on Web Services, New York, pp. 607–614 (2015). https://doi.org/10.1109/ICWS.201 5.86

10. Uakarn, C., Chaokromthong, K., Sintao, N.: Sample size estimation using Yamane and Cochran and Krejcie and Morgan and green formulas and Cohen statistical power analysis by G*power and comparisons. Apheit Int. J. **10**(2), 76–88 (2021)

11. Liengaard, B.D., Sharma, P.N., Hult, G.T.M., Jensen, M.B., Sarstedt, M., Hair, J.F., et al.: Prediction: coveted, yet forsaken? introducing a cross- validated predictive ability test in partial least squares path modeling. Decis. Sci. **52**, 362–392 (2021). https://doi.org/10.1111/deci.12445

12. Del-Castillo-Feito, C., Cachón-Rodríguez, G., Paz-Gil, I.: Political Disaffection, Sociodemographic, and Psychographic Variables as State Legitimacy Determinants in the European Union. Thousand Oaks CA: American Behavioral Scientist, Del-Castil (2020)

13. Cachón-Rodríguez, G., Blanco-González, A., Prado-Román, C., and Diez-Martin, F. (2021). Sustainability actions, employee loyalty, and the awareness: the mediating effect of organization legitimacy. Manage. Decis. Econ. **42**(7), 1730–1739 (2021). https://doi.org/10.1002/mde.3340

14. Hair, J.F., Risher, J.J., Sarstedt, M., Ringle, C.M.: When to use and how to report the results of PLS-SEM. Eur. Bus. Rev. **31**, 2–24 (2019). https://doi.org/10.1108/ebr-11-2018-0203

15. Martínez-Navalón, J., Gelashvili, V., Gómez-Ortega, A.: Evaluation of user satisfaction and trust of review platforms: analysis of the impact of privacy and E-WOM in the case of tripadvisor. Front. Psychol. **12**, 750527 (2021). https://doi.org/10.3389/fpsyg.2021.750527

16. INEC, Census of population and housing. https://www.ecuadorencifras.gob.ec/censo-de-poblacion-y-vivienda/. Accessed 04 Nov 2022

17. Yoon, J.E.: A Study on User Perception and Use Intention of Digital Content Characteristics. Kyonggi University Graduate School, Ph.D. thesis (2006)

18. Smith, J., Johnson, A.: Examining customer satisfaction using a likert scale: a case study of the hospitality industry. J. Cons. Behavior **15**(3), 123–145 (2020). https://doi.org/10.1002/cb.12345

19. Rodríguez, G.C., Román, C.P., Zúñiga-Vicente, J.Á.: The relationship between identification and loyalty in a public university: are there differences between (the perceptions) professors and graduates? Eur. Res. Manage. Bus. Econ. **25**, 122–128 (2019). https://doi.org/10.1016/j.iedeen.2019.04.005

20. Carmines, E., Zeller, R.: Reliability and Validity Assessment. Sage, Thousand Oaks CA (1979)

21. Hair, J.F., Hult, G.T.M., Ringle, C.M., Sarstedt, M.: A Primer on Partial Least Squares Structural Equation Modeling (PLS-SEM). Sage Publications (2017)

22. Martínez-Navalón, J.G., Gelashvili, V., Saura, J.R.: The impact of environmental social media publications on user satisfaction with and trust in tourism businesses. Environ. Res. Public Health **17**, 5417 (2020). https://doi.org/10.3390/ijerph17155417

23. Dijkstra, T.K., Henseler, J.: Consistent partial least squares path modeling. MIS Q. **39**, 297–316 (2015)

24. Ghasemy, M., Muhammad, F., Jamali, J., Roldán, J.L.: Satisfaction and performance of the international faculty: to what extent emotional reactions and conflict matter? SAGE Open **11**, 1–15 (2021). https://doi.org/10.1177/21582440211030598

25. Henseler, J., Ringle, C.M., Sarstedt, M.: A new criterion for assessing discriminant validity in variance-based structural equation modeling. J. Acad. Market Sci. **43**, 115–135 (2015). https://doi.org/10.1007/s11747-014-0403-8

26. Aldás-Manzano, M.J.: Confirmatory tetrad analysis as a tool to decide between the formative/reflective nature of constructs in marketing and management research. In: Moutinho, A.K., Bigné, L., Manrai, E., (eds.). Routledge Companion to the Future of Marketing, (Milton Park: Routledge), pp. 348–378 (2014)

27. Cohen, J., Cohen, P., West, S.G., Aiken, L.S.: Applied Multiple Regression/Correlation Analysis for the Behavioral Sciences (3rd ed.). Lawrence Erlbaum Associates (2003)

Correction to: Evaluating Perceived Value and Intention to Continue Using Over-the-Top Services in Latin America: A Case Study in Quito, Ecuador

Carina Haro Granizo(iD) and Gonzalo Olmedo(iD)

Correction to:
Chapter 10 in: M. J. Abásolo et al. (Eds.): *Applications*
and Usability of Interactive TV, **CCIS 1820,**
https://doi.org/10.1007/978-3-031-45611-4_10

The original version of this chapter was revised: The corresponding author Haro Granizo Carina affiliation (address: Universidad de las Fuerzas Armadas ESPE, Sangolquí, Ecuador; ORCID: 0000-0002-4918-2349) and co-author Olmedo Gonzalo affiliation (address: WiCOM-Energy Research Group, Department of Electrical, Electronics, and Telecommunications, Universidad de las Fuerzas Armadas ESPE, Sangolquí, Ecuador; ORCID: 0000-0002-6205-1685) has been updated.

The updated version of this chapter can be found at
https://doi.org/10.1007/978-3-031-45611-4_10

Author Index

M. J. Abásolo et al. (Eds.): jAUTI 2022, CCIS 1820, p. 161, 2023.
https://doi.org/10.1007/978-3-031-45611-4

Author Index

Printed in the United States
by Baker & Taylor Publisher Services

Printed in the United States
by Baker & Taylor Publisher Services